ENGLISH QUANTIFIERS:
LOGICAL STRUCTURE AND
LINGUISTIC VARIATION

Taishukan Studies in Modern Linguistics
Susumu Kuno and Kinsuke Hasegawa, Editors

ENGLISH QUANTIFIERS

logical structure and linguistic variation

Guy Carden Yale University

ACADEMIC PRESS   1976

New York   San Francisco   London

A Subsidiary of Harcourt Brace Jovanovich, Publishers

ACADEMIC PRESS, INC.
111 Fifth Avenue, New York, New York 10003

ACADEMIC PRESS, INC. (LONDON) LTD.
24/28 Oval Road, London NW1

Library of Congress Catalog Card Number: 76-24155

ISBN: 0-12-159350-9

PE
1199
C37
1976

PRINTED IN JAPAN

Acknowledgements

This book is a revised and slightly expanded version of a thesis presented to the Department of Linguistics of Harvard University, June 1970, under the title *Logical Predicates and Idiolect Variation in English*. The major part of the writing was done while I was stationed at the Air Force Cambridge Research Laboratories, Applied Mathematics Branch, Data Sciences Laboratory (1969–71). My earlier work in syntax was supported by the National Science Foundation under grants GN 329 and GN 554 to Harvard University (1966–67) and by a research assistantship at the IBM Boston Programming Center (summer 1967). I am grateful to these institutions for their support, and to my supervisors— Robert M. Alexander (LR), Susumu Kuno (Harvard), John Moyne (IBM), and Rocco H. Urbano (LRA)—for their advice and encouragement.

Some sixty or seventy remarkably patient informants endured a long cross-examination while I was gathering data; I take this opportunity to thank them collectively.

My teachers and my fellow students at Harvard, MIT, and Brandeis have contributed to this book directly and indirectly; I should mention especially tutorials in descriptive and historical linguistics with Professors Robert Underhill and Calvert Watkins and discussions about syntax with Ray Jackendoff and Brian Sinclair. My teachers in syntax, of course, have made the greatest contribution: Professors George Lakoff, David Perlmutter, and John Robert Ross will recognize the results of their teaching and criticism at many points.

My greatest debt is to Professor Susumu Kuno. In 1966 he suggested this research topic to me; and since then he has been most generous with his time, guiding my work with insightful comments and criticisms and devastating counter-examples. His advice and encouragement have been vital to the completion of this book.

My mistakes, of course, are my own; and the people who have helped and advised me do not necessarily agree with anything I say.

Chapters 2, 3, and 5 first appeared in a slightly different form in *Linguistic Inquiry*, Volume 1, Numbers 3 and 4 (1970); and Appendix B first appeared in *Papers from the Sixth Regional Meeting of the Chicago Linguistic Society*. These papers are reprinted by permission of the MIT Press and the Chicago Linguistic Society.

Table of Contents

Introduction:
Logical Structure and
Linguistic Variation[1]

1. Objectives

This book has two main objectives: 1. To present and defend an analysis of the underlying structure of quantifiers. 2. To develop a new method of proof based on linguistic variation. These two goals are inter-dependent, since the best arguments for the proposed quantifier analysis are based on linguistic variation, and the proposed methodology is exemplified and shown to be useful by application to the quantifier problem.

---

[1] An Introduction saying what this book purports to accomplish cries out for a footnote explaining what this book does not purport to accomplish:

—By "quantifiers" I mean "all," "every," "each," "many," "few," "much," and "little," though it appears that much of the analysis will also apply to generics and number words. "Some," "any," "no," "none," "not a," "not one," etc. have been deliberately excluded because of the problems involved with the putative *some-any* rule. (See Klima (1964b), Carden (1968b), and R. Lakoff (1969b) for examples of the problems that arise.) When this difficulty is straightened out, I would expect this group to form a natural class with the quantifiers listed above.

—I do not discuss the details of the possible surface structure for quantifiers; see footnote 16.1 to Chapter 1. Similarly, I do not discuss the details of the various late quantifier and NEG moving rules; these were discussed at length in my MA thesis (Carden 1968a).

—The phenomena I have considered do not force me to distinguish between partitive and non-partitive uses of quantifiers ("many men" vs "many of the men"); I regard the correct solution for this problem as an open question.

—I do not wish to give the impression that I have "solved" quantifiers; a great number of problems remain unsolved. It would be fair to say that this book raises more questions than it answers.

2. Preliminaries

I assume that the reader is familiar with the transformational literature up to Katz and Postal (1964) and Chomsky (1965); I take their model for language as a starting point, and introduce changes and additional references as needed. I therefore begin with a system of "meaning-preserving syntax" where "deep structure" is the input to an ordered set of transformational rules that do not change meaning. Literal meaning[2] is fully determined by deep structure, and nonsynonymous sentences must have distinct deep structures. I do not exclude the possibility that some synonymous sentences may have distinct deep structures related to a single semantic structure by interpretive rules.

I should warn the reader that I use the term "deep structure" in an idiosyncratic way, distinct from the usage of Chomsky (1965). At present I consider it an open question whether there is a singnificant linguistic level between semantic structure and shallow structure. I therefore use "deep structure" to mean the deepest level of underlying structure motivated by existing evidence, but I do not rule out the possibility that additional evidence may show that this structure is itself transformationally derived from a deeper one. It is thus quite possible that my deep structures represent only successive approximations to semantic structure.

Since 1965 it has become clear that the simple meaning-preserving-syntax model of language has to be substantially modified, and there is a continuing controversy as to the form of modification required. The major competing proposals are:

1. Interpretive Semantics, supported by Chomsky (e.g. 1970) and best exemplified in the work of Jackendoff (1969 ab, 1972).
2. Generative Semantics, exemplified by the work of Lakoff, McCawley, and Postal (see Bibliography).

Points of controversy include lexical decomposition, the existence of a level of deep structure in the sense of Chomsky (1965), the formal mechanisms permitted for syntactic and semantic rules, and the abstractness of underlying structure. The evidence I give here bears primarily on the abstractness issue, and supports the generative semantics model.

---

[2] "Literal meaning" includes basic grammatical relations like subject-verb and logical relations like relative scope of quantifiers; a wider concept of meaning would also consider appropriate contexts, presuppositions, entailment, etc.

3. The Logical-Structure Controversy

Consider the problem of logical structure in natural language: Is there a "natural logic"? What elements in natural language perform the functions of the quantifiers, negatives, predicates, and variables of formal logic? What is their underlying structure? How do they interact?

These questions about logical structure have become one of the focal points of the interpretive/generative semantics controversy. There are two main reasons for the special attention given to logical structure:

1. It is clear that the English translations of logical elements—words like *and*, *all*, and *not*—do not fit comfortably into the meaning-preserving-syntax model for language (see Chapter 1 for examples of the problems that arise). Logical structure, therefore, is a point where both sides agree that the old model will have to be changed.

2. Thanks to the work of logicians, it is reasonably clear how logical relations should be represented in semantic structure. Both sides appear to agree that this component of meaning can be represented by a notation essentially equivalent to predicate calculus.[3]

These underlying agreements make it possible to focus on two key issues: formal mechanisms and abstractness of underlying structure. The competing proposals can be summarized as follows:

1. Interpetive Semantics : (see Jackendoff 1968 ab, 1969 b, 1971, 1972 ; Partee 1970) Deep structure is relatively close to surface structures, so that logical elements appear in roughly the same structures in deep and in surface structure (for example, base rules generate quantifiers as elements of the noun phrases they modify). Logical relations are not defined in deep structure ; instead, logical relations are determined by semantic interpretation rules that apply to surface structure. These "surface-structure interpretation rules" thus map surface structure into semantic representation.

2. Generative Semantics: (see Lakoff 1965, 1969, 1970 ab; Carden 1968 a) Deep structure is relatively abstract, and logical elements appear in markedly different structures in deep and in surface structure (for example, quantifiers are predicates of higher sentences in deep structure). Logical relations are explicitly marked in deep structure, which requires a system of "derivational constraints" to control the application of transformations.

---

[3] This is explicit in the work of generative semanticists like Lakoff, but only implicit in interpretive analyses like Jackendoff (1969a).

The logical-structure part of the generative/interpretive semantics controversy therefore boils down to two issues: (1) abstractness of deep structure. (2) Formal mechanisms—surface-structure interpretation rules *vs* derivational constraints.

The evidence I give in this book bears primarily on the abstractness issue, and only indirectly on the formal-mechanism issue. I argue that quantifiers (Chapters 1, 3, and 4) and conjuctions (Appendix B) appear in deep structure as the predicates of higher sentences, so that logical relations are explicitly marked in deep structure, as claimed by the generative-semantics model. This analysis in turn indirectly supports the generative-semantics position on formal mechanisms: if logical relations are explicitly marked in deep structure, it is redundant to have surface-structure interpretation rules whose only function is to re-determine these logical relations.[4]

4. The Problem of Linguistic Variation

Languages differ from each other; within a given language there are typically both regional and social dialects; within a given speech-community the idiolects of the individual speakers will differ; and a given speaker will typically have several different styles of speaking and writing. Transformational grammarians have generally held that a synchronic linguistic description should abstract away from the range of linguistic variation within a given language and describe only an idealized, uniform dialect. Chomsky's view in *Aspects* (1965) is typical:

> "Linguistic theory is concerned primarily with an ideal speaker-listener, in a perfectly homogeneous speech-community, . . ." (p. 3)

The procedure has been to describe one dialect at a time, without using any evidence from related dialects, and ignoring any variation within the dialect under study. This single-dialect approach is based on the assumption that the variations within a properly chosen dialect will be insignificant, so that the grammar will be essentially the same whichever of the variants we choose to describe. It has even been suggested (Katz and Fodor 1963) that anything

---

[4] Of course this argument ignores the question of independent motivation for derivational constraints. While examples involving logical relations seem to show a near stand-off between derivational constraints and surface-structure interpretation rules (Chapter 5 gives one such example), recent work (e.g. Andrews 1971, Lakoff 1970e) suggests that derivational constraints will be needed for purely syntactic operations like case marking. As long as surface-structure interpretation rules lack equivalent independent motivation, this evidence must be decisive for the formal-mechanism issue.

informants disagree about is, *ipso facto*, outside the subject matter of synchronic linguistics:

> "The generalization is this: *If speakers can employ an ability in apprehending the structure of any sentence in the infinite set of sentences of a language without reference to information about settings and without significant variation from speaker to speaker, then that ability is properly the subject matter of a synchronic theory in linguistics.*"   (p. 484, emphasis in original)

A model that *a priori* rules out consideration of linguistic variation has obvious advantages: Field work can be limited to a very few informants; or the linguist himself can serve as the sole informant.[5] The idealization is convenient, but we must ask if it is safe: Are the disagreements among informants in a given speech community always either insignificant or concerned with matters properly outside the area of synchronic linguistics?

At least in the area of syntax and semantics, the answer is no. Informants from the same speech-community, even from the same family, often disagree sharply on the meaning and grammaticality of test sentences. These disagreements are not limited to insignificant cases, but seem to be equally likely when the sentence is a crucial test for some major theoretical issue. If we use the standard single-dialect approach, we have two choices:

1.   We can say that the disagreeing informants speak separate dialects, each of which must be described without reference to the other. But when informants A and B speak superficially similar dialects of American English, we must be suspicious of a theory that forces us to conclude that Informant A speaks a language with, say, deep structure and interpretive semantic rules, while Informant B speaks a language with a generative semantics controlled by derivational constraints. Is it merely a coincidence that A and B can understand each other?

2.   We can rule out the data about which the informants disagree, as the Katz and Fodor quotation suggests. But then we must conclude that informant judgments of grammaticality and meaning are not part of the subject matter of synchronic linguistics. This would require that we abandon almost all the recent work in syntax and semantics.

---

[5] This is, of course, a very risky procedure, since working on a problem is likely to distort the linguist's intuitions; I have long been completely untrustworthy as an informant on sentences containing quantifiers or negatives. Linguists who have not been working on a particular problem, on the other hand, are often very good informants, requiring little if any training.

4.1 The Unified-Analysis Approach

To avoid the difficulties mentioned in the preceding section, we must find
a way to account for the variation; that is, we must find an analysis that displays
both the similarities and the differences among the dialects, and thus accounts
both for the fact that the informants can usually understand each other and
for the relatively rare cases where there are misunderstandings.

This problem has been attacked, usually for phonological dialects, in both
the structuralist and generative traditions. The Trager-Smith overall pattern
(1951), the Weinreich diasystem (1954), Hockett's common core (1955), De
Camp's conversion rules (1963), Bailey's polylectal analysis (1969), and the
transformational analyses using rule order (Halle 1962, Keyser 1963, Klima
1964 a) are all attempts to find an insightful representation of dialect variation.

In this book I argue that the sort of dialect variation we find in syntax and
semantics requires a further step. It is not enough to analyze the dialects independently, and then find a formal way of representing the differences. Instead
we must consider all the available dialect evidence when doing the analysis, and
seek an analysis in which the dialects differ minimally.[6] That is, the variation
itself becomes part of the relevant evidence in choosing among analyses. This
is not an entirely new idea: Stockwell (1959) suggests that the analyst could
choose the phonemicization that "integrates most easily into the inventory
of the over-all pattern"; and Saporta (1965) shows that an independent analysis
of Castilian and Uruguayan plural formation gives absurd results, and argues
that a unified analysis is required. In Carden (1970, 1973), I suggest a general
methodology in which one seeks a "unified analysis" for conflicting idiolects.

The need for a unified analysis is especially clear in the syntactic/semantic
dialects I discuss in this book. The dialects discussed by the structural dialec-
tologists, though they could be defined in linguistic terms, correlated with some
independently determined sociological characteristic of speakers (class, education,
geographical origin), so that one could speak of a "Yorkshire dialect" or a "lower-
middle class dialect." When we look at my informant responses, the informants
fall into linguistically-defined groups, with only some of the mathematically
possible combinations of responses appearing (see Chapter 4). These groups,

---

[6] One has a certain feel for big and little differences between grammars, and the cases that
have come up to date have had clear solutions; still, it will plainly be necessary to search for
a structural definition of "differ minimally." For example, one might be able to find a
hierarchy of types of structural difference, from those that distinguished languages to
those that represented free variation in an individual speaker. Such a hierarchy could
then be used to rank-order differences between grammars.

however, seem to be randomly distributed with respect to the sociological characteristics of the informants, with members of the same nuclear family falling into two or even three of the dialects.[7] This random distribution of dialects makes it especially implausible that they should have gross structural differences, and supports the unified-analysis proposal. Of course the ideal analysis would include a mechanism by which the random distribution could arise; one such suggestion is made in Chapter 4.

Essentially the same form of dialect-variation argument that I apply to quantifiers (Chapter 3) and the scope problem (Chapter 5) has been applied to a fair variety of problems in the recent literature: *do so* (Bailey 1970b), Catalan vowel reduction (Vogt 1971), *Not*-Transportation (Carden 1971), and the relation between negative-polarity items and VP anaphora (Grinder and Postal 1971, p 306).

4.2 Data Collection

The dialect-variation data reported in Chapters 3 and 4 is based on open-ended interviews with sixty informants, who were asked to judge the grammaticality and meaning of orally presented sentences. The data in the other chapters is based on informal sentence-checking with a relatively small number of informants.

4.2.1 The Informant

The informants were selected on the basis of convenience, and are not in any sense a random sample. With a few exceptions, they were college-educated, middle-class, and either natives or long-time inhabitants of the North-Eastern United States.

1. *Training the Informant:* The first interview with a naive (non-linguist) informant began with a training period in which I explained to the informant what the purpose of the study was, what sort of judgment he was supposed to make, and what sorts of information it would be useful for him to volunteer.

2. *Defining the Task:* Terms like "grammatical," "unacceptable," "semantically anomalous," "grammatical but stylistically infelicitous" are reasonably clear to a linguist, but worse than meaningless to the new informant. It is of no

[7] It has been suggested that, because of this random distribution, the term "dialect" is unsuitable. While it would be possible to manufacture some term like "idiolect cluster" (IC) to describe the objects we are concerned with, it seems preferable to reduce the proliferation of terminology and maintain the term "dialect" to mean a linguistically defined grouping of idiolects. This usage has been standard in the transformationalist literature.

value to know that 13 informants find sentence (8) "grammatical" unless you
know they mean the same thing by "grammatical." My first step was to explain
that I was not interested in grade-school "grammaticality," that I was dealing
with examples that different people used differently, so that I was interested in
what the informant would say himself, not in what other people might say. At this
stage it proved helpful to give a series of sentences unrelated to the constructions
being studied, choosing examples where I was reasonably sure of the informant's
"right" reaction. British dialects were a good source of starred examples for
American informants:

(1)   a.   Give it me!
      b.   Do you want it mending?
      c.   Q.   Will the medicine help the patient?
           A.   It might do.

In discussing such examples, the informant gets an idea of what he is expected
to do, how to locate the problem with a bad sentence, and how to describe what
a sentence means (paraphrase is probably the best technique). This training
period also helped me to standardize the coding for the rest of the interview,
since I got a feel for the informant's responses to sentences of known grammaticality.

4.2.2 The Interview

1. *Interview Setting:* In almost all cases, informants were interviwed
separately. When a group interview was necessary, it was helpful to make sure
all the informants had made up their minds before the first gave his response;
people can be astonishingly sheep-like.

Being an informant is very tiring; they find that after a while all sentences
begin to sound alike. Also, if the informant hears similar constructions in quick
succession, his remembered response to the previous sentence influences his
response to the current one. For both these reasons, I preferred several short
interviews with a given informant to one long one. Repeating interviews also
gave a chance to check on test-retest reliability. When a single long interview was
necessary, as it often was, separating occurrences of similar constructions and
providing rest periods proved helpful.

2. *Presenting the Test Sentence:* In this study, I have tried to find all the
possible meanings the written sentence shown in the text could have. In many
cases, a particular stress or intonation pattern will enforce one reading or another;
I therefore presented the test sentence several times during the discussion, initially with a "neutral" pattern, and then with patterns known to enforce various

readings for other informants. It was common for the informant to report that the written or "neutral" version of the sentence was unambiguous, but suddenly notice another reading when the sentence was repeated with a new pattern. My results are therefore biased in the direction of finding sentences maximally ambiguous.

3. *Coding Responses:* Informants' judgments on grammaticality have been recorded on a three point scale: "OK," "?" (doubtful acceptability), and "*" (not acceptable). The problem is to interpret the informants' responses so that these symbols are assigned uniformly from informant to informant. The informants' responses to the training sentences were a help in standardization, but a considerable judgment factor remains. I have tried to make the cuts at points where the informant reported a clear difference in acceptability without too much regard for the words he used to describe the absolute acceptability. That is, I have tried to establish a comparative scale based on differences in acceptability, rather than an absolute scale.

Coding judgments on meaning was usually simpler, though I often had to ask for several paraphrases before being sure of the intended meaning. Sometimes a more structured question of the form "Would it be synonymous with— or with—?" was needed.

4. *Focusing on a particular construction:* Initially, the informant evaluates the test sentence as a whole; if he accepts the sentence, then *a fortiori* he accepts the construction being tested. If he rejects the sentence, however, the interviewer must make sure he is rejecting the construction under test and not some other part of the sentence. Of course one tries to construct examples so the only questionable part is the one being tested, but informants often surprise you. One informant rejected all imperatives; "Why?" "Oh, I'd say 'please'." Various methods were used to locate the source of the problem: "How would *you* phrase it?" "What seems to be the problem?" "How would you change the sentence to make it mean ——?" Simply asking the informant to repeat the sentence often helped locate the problem. The informant can often identify the problem by similarity if not more specificly: "It's got the same thing wrong with it as ——." Unfortunately responses of this sort are hard to elicit without leading questions.

4.2.3 Reliability and Validity

1. *How Many Informants?:* One naturally distrusts any dialect attested by only a single informant, since he might have misunderstood the task, been tired, answered facetiously, etc. Two informants are much more than twice as good as one, and a dialect with three informants can be regarded as reasonably well established. A harder question is when you can assume you have enough

informants to have caught all the significant "randomly" distributed dialects. Lacking statistical information on the actual nature of the distribution, we are forced to guess: Perhaps fewer than ten might suffice if the informants were unanimous and confident; my twenty-five informants for Chapter 4 are almost certainly too few for that complicated situation.

2. *Interview vs Questionnaire:* If you could use questionnaires instead of time-consuming individual interviews, you could get a far larger sample of informants for an equal amount of work. Questionnaires would have the further advantage that the instructions and sample sentences could be presented completely uniformly to all informants (a similar advantage could be obtained by using a tape recorder to present instructions and test sentences in an interview).

Unfortunately, my experience pre-testing questionnaires on syntax and semantics shows that the informant training, coding, and focusing problems described in the preceding sections make questionnaires impractical. While these problems can be handled fairly easily in interaction with an informant, a questionnaire that tries to handle them becomes an essay in linguistics that only an unusually intelligent informant can understand, and only an unusually patient one will read.

It has been pointed out (e.g. Heringer 1970) that there is a danger that the linguist-informant interaction will bias the results, with the informants' answers being influenced by clues picked up from the interviewer. While this is certainly a problem that the interviewer must be constantly aware of, it is not a problem that can be solved by the use of questionnaires, since the same possibility for biasing the results appears in the wording of the questions and instructions.

3. *Validity:* Given that we want to find out about the nature of human language, are we right to investigate informants' intuitive judgments of meaning and grammaticality, as transformational grammarians have almost invariably done? Labov (1970, 1972, Chap. 8) argues that we are wrong, and that a direct study of performance is more valid; and he backs his arguments with some very impressive research results (e.g. Labov et al 1968). Labov's arguments merit serious study and further research, but at present I do not see any alternative to the use of intuitive judgments in research on delicate syntactic/semantic questions of the sort I discuss here.

4. *Test-Retest Reliability:* If I asked my informants again tomorrow, would they give me the same answers? While the interview procedure was not specifically designed to check the stability of the dialects, a certain amount of re-testing was done in the course of the interviewing. The results show a reasonable test-retest reliability: out of 125 examples, there were a maximum of 15 unexplained

changes, or about 88% reliability.[8]

5. Plan of the Book

Chapters 1 and 2 present the initial motivation for the proposed analysis of quantifiers. I argue that quantifiers appear as predicates in underlying structure, and that these predicates appear in two distinct structures: 1. A "higher-S" underlying structure, which leads to "pre-determiner" surface structures like "every boy" or "many of the men" (Chapter 1). 2. An underlying structure identical to that of non-restrictive adjectives, which leads to "post-determiner" surface structures like "the many men" (Chapter 2).

Chapter 3 introduces the dialect-variation method of argument. The evidence shows that idiolects of English do not vary unpredictably or without limit; instead they fall into linguistically-defined groups or clusters that I shall call "dialects." I argue that a linguistic description should not confine itself to one idiolect or dialect, but that there is an obligation to seek an analysis in which the mutually comprehensible dialects of a given language differ minimally. I then apply this principle to three well-defined quantifier dialects, and show that the higher-S analysis proposed in Chapter 1 makes it possible to explain all three dialects in a unified way, using independently motivated constraints.

Chapters 4 and 5 tie up loose ends from Chapter 3 while bringing out additional points about dialect variation. In Chapter 4 I consider sub-dialects within the most important quantifier dialect, and show that these sub-dialects can be accounted for by differences in rule ordering. This in turn leads to a concept of attested, possible, and impossible sub-dialects. In Chapter 5 we consider the problem of scope determination, and see that the Jackendoff and Lakoff proposals have a common flaw. While the evidence does not lead to a clear solution, it appears that an argument combining dialect-variation evidence with an historically-motivated theory of linguistic change will be crucial to the eventual solution. This offers an interesting approach to the problem of the synchronic relevance of diachronic evidence.

---

[8] The 15 unexplained changes are dividied into six cases of possible coding errors (e.g. one response coded "?" and one coded "?*") and nine totally unexplained. In addition there were nine cases of interviewer error (mostly failure to present a needed intonation pattern) and two cases of systematic change under pressure (NEG-Q speakers changed to AMB after some months' exposure to sentences grammatical only on a NEG-V reading, cf. Chapter 3.). This reasonably good reliability is in sharp contrast to the results of Labov (1970) on intuitive judgments; the discrepancy may be caused by differences in methodology or in the constructions under study.

Two appendices develop points peripheral to the main argument. Appendix A shows that the NP-identity analysis of Reflexive leads to an ordering paradox much like the one Postal (1970) discovered for the equivalent analysis of Equi-NP Deletion. This adds weight to the evidence, from Bach's Paradox (Bach 1970) on, that we shall need an entirely new approach to anaphora. Appendix B considers "both," which at first glance appears to be a quantifier, and shows that it actually must be derived from an underlying sentence conjunction. The similarities that appear between quantifiers and conjunctions suggests the admittedly speculative conclusion that they, together with negatives, form an underlying class of "logical predicates." The appendices thus point out two promising directions for future research.

Chapter 1:

The Underlying Structure of Pre-Determiner Quantifiers

1. Introduction

In early work in generative grammar,[1] it was assumed that a quantifier phrase like "every optimist" formed a single constituent in both deep and surface structure, with the quantifier itself analyzed as part of a determiner or pre-determiner sub-constituent. In this chapter I give initial motivation for a revision of this analysis.

We notice first that NPs modified by quantifiers act unlike other NPs in examples with anaphora rules like Equi-NP Deletion,[2] suggesting that the structure of quantifier phrases should be significantly different from that of other NPs. Looking for evidence as to what this difference might be, we investigate the interaction of quantifiers and negation, in particular the rule of *Not*-Transportation (NT).[2] We find that, here too, quantifiers behave in an apparently anomalous fashion, but that the anomaly can be explained by an independently-motivated generalization about NT if the quantifier is in some sense in a "higher S" at the time the NT rule applies.

This suggests a revised analysis of quantifiers, in which a pre-determiner quantifier like "every" appears in underlying structure in a "higher S" (S_0 in the tree[3] below) that dominates the S_1 in which the quantifier appears in surface

---

[1] See, for example, discussion in Lakoff (1965 p F23) and Jackendoff (1968a pp 5–13).

[2] For discussion of Equi-NP Deletion, see section 2 of this chapter, Lakoff (1965 pp V3 A20, F4), and Jackendoff (1971 p 282). For discussion of *Not*-Transportation, see section 3.1 of this chapter and the references listed in footnote 7 there.

[3] All tree diagrams are much simplified and omit any structure that is not relevant to the points under discussion. Omitted structure is indicated by a triangle, as in NP_q in this tree.

structure. A rule of Quantifier-Lowering (QL) will then be required to move the quantifier from this higher S into its surface-structure position as a constituent of the NP it modifies.

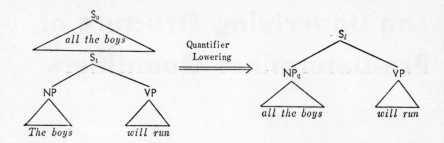

Considerations of deep-structure simplicity make it possible to assign some internal structure to this higher S_0, but these conclusions are only weakly supported, and must be regarded as a first approximation to the correct sturcture.

This higher-S analysis, motivated by the wish to preserve a generalization about the application of NT, turns out in addition to explain the behavior of quantifiers in certain Equi-NP Deletion sentences, at least within the limits of our present understanding of anaphora. The first-approximation analysis given here will be developed and applied in the later chapters, where additional confirming evidence will be presented.

2. A Counter-Example to the Usual Analysis

Lakoff and Bach have independently pointed out that sentences like (la) and (lb) are not synonymous and so must be derived from different deep structures:

> (1) a. Every optimist expects every optimist to be President. $\neq$
>   b. Every optimist expects to be President.

Sentences with generics share this property.[4]

> (2) a. A Senator expects a Senator to be treated with respect. $\neq$
>   b. A Senator expects to be treated with respect.

Consider a deep structure reflecting the usual analysis where "every optimist"

---

[4] Brian Sinclair, Ray Jackendoff, and Richard Miller have independently pointed this out. Examples like (2) suggest the generalization that generics and quantifiers, which form a semantic class, also form a syntactic class; Miller (1967) gives additional evidence for this hypothesis.

or "a Senator" forms an NP in deep structure:

(1′)

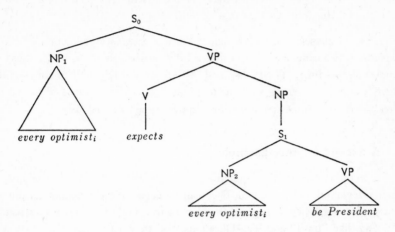

Since both occurrences of "every optimist" refer to the same people, (1′) must reduce to (lb) on the pattern of (3):

(3)   a.   *John$_i$ expects John$_i$ to be President. $\xrightarrow{\text{oblig. Equi-NP Deletion}}$
        b.   John$_i$ expects to be President.

It follows that (1′) is the deep structure of (lb), and we have no way to generate (la). It is no help to make an *ad hoc* rule that Equi-NP Deletion is blocked for "quantifier and generic phrases," since then we could get (la) but not (lb). If we make Equi-NP Deletion optional for quantifier phrases, we should then get (la) and (lb) from the same deep structure (1′), which is wrong since they are not synonymous.

Similar problems arise in sentences involving pronouns and reflexives:

(4)   a.   Every optimist$_i$ admires every optimist$_i$.
        b.   Every optimist admires himself.

(5)   a.   *John$_i$ admires John$_i$. $\xrightarrow{\text{oblig. Reflexive}}$
        b.   John admires himself.

Here (4a) and (4b) are not synonymous, and must therefore have distinct deep structures. But we must then find some principled way to prevent (4a) from reducing to (4b) on the pattern of (5), and likewise we must find some way to generate the reflexive pronoun in (4b) starting from some structure distinct from (4a). Exactly the same arguments hold for examples with pronominalization:

$(4')$ a.   Every optimist$_i$ expects that every optimist$_i$ will win.

   b.   Every optimist$_i$ expects that he$_i$ will win.

$(5')$ a.   *John$_i$ expects that John$_i$ will win. $\xrightarrow{\text{oblig. Pronominalization}}$

   b.   John$_i$ expects that he$_i$ will win.

Given the present uncertainty about the way anaphora phenomena are to be explained,[5] we cannot expect to find a fully satisfactory solution for these examples at this time. (1), (2), (4), and (4') are primarily useful to show us that there is something wrong with the usual analysis of quantifiers, and to make us alert for other cases where quantifiers appear to act anomalously.

3. A Second Counter-Example

Noun phrases containing quantifiers also appear to behave anomalously in their interaction with negation. They can be negated independently of the rest of the sentence, when so negated they have curious effects on polarity-sensitive[6] elements like "until" and Tag-Questions, and they act irregularly under *Not*-Transportation. In this section we shall be primarily concerned with their behavior under *Not*-Transportation.

3.1 *Not*-Transportation

Consider sentences like (6):

(6)   a.   John thinks the boys didn't leave.

   b.   John doesn't think the boys left.

It has long been known that sentences like (6b) have a reading synonymous with (6a); it has been usual to account for this by a minor rule of *Not*-Transportation (NT) that, for certain /+NT/ verbs like "think," moves a negative from the embedded sentence ("the boys didn't leave") to the verb of the higher sentence ("thinks"). This *Not*-Transportation analysis is supported by various persuasive syntactic and semantic arguments.[7]

The most familiar, though not necessarily the most persuasive, of these arguments involves "until" adverbials. These appear with point-action predicates like "leave" or "catch the train" only when either the predicate or the adverbial

---

[5] See Appendix A for a discussion of various problems with anaphora.

[6] In the sense of Baker (1970b).

[7] The *Not*-Transportation rule is due originally to Fillmore (1963); see R. Lakoff (1969a), G. Lakoff (1970c), Jackendoff (1971), and Carden (1971) for discussions of the current controversy about this rule.

is negative in underlying structure:

(7) a.   John didn't leave until Friday.
     b.   *John left until Friday.

Sentences like (7b), however, are grammatical if they are embedded under a negative $/+NT/$ verb:

(8) a.   Bill doesn't think John will leave until Friday.
     b.   Bill thinks John won't leave until Friday.

We conclude that there is a generalization in saying that the same constraint applies to (8) as to (7), and that (8a) is derived transformationally from (8b), where the point-action predicate "leave" is overtly negative.

Consider now what happens when the embedded S is itself complex, as in (9):

(9) a.   John doesn't think the boys who left will catch the train.
     b.   John thinks that the boys who left won't catch the train.
     c.   John thinks that the boys who didn't leave will catch the train.
(9') John thinks the boys who left will catch the train.

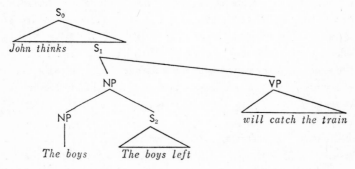

(9a) has a reading synonymous with (9b), but no reading synonymous with (9c). It follows that, in the deep structure of the reading under consideration, there was a negative on "catch" in S_1 and no negative on "leave" in S_2. The generalization, at least for cases where the verb of the highest embedded S is, like "catch," $/-NT/$, is that *Not*-Transportation can take a negative only from the topmost S embedded under a $/+NT/$ verb.

3.2   Negatives and Quantifiers

Notice that a quantifier can be negated independently of the main verb in its sentence:

(10) a.   Not all the boys will run.

b. All the boys won't run.

NEG-Q Reading: $\sim((\forall x_\varepsilon \text{ the boys}) (\text{will run}(x)))$

NEG-V Reading: $(\forall x_\varepsilon \text{ the boys}) (\sim (\text{will run}(x)))$

Early standard analyses that were not concerned with meaning (e.g. Klima 1964b) derived sentences like (10 a) and (10 b) from a common underlying structure like (Fig. 1):

Fig. 1

Sentence-Negation Deep Structure for (10 a b)

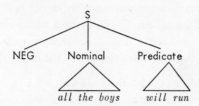

In such an analysis, a series of transformational rules would apply to Fig. 1, optionally moving the sentence-negation "neg" into the predicate (NEG-Placement, producing 10 b) or attaching it to the quantifier (Klima's "neg-incorporation into indefinites," producing 10 a).

Consider now the meanings of (10 a b). (10 a) has only the NEG-Q reading, where the negation is construed with the quantifier "all." In the dialect we are concerned with,[8] (10 b) is ambiguous between the NEG-Q reading and the NEG-V reading, where the negative is construed with the predicate "will run."

Given the meaning-preserving syntax hypothesis, the NEG-V reading cannot have the same deep structure as the NEG-Q reading. It follows that we shall have to modify the standard analyses in which (10 a) and (10 b) were derived from a single underlying structure like Fig. 1. From the evidence of (10 a b), we already know some of the requirements for the new analysis: A. There must be separate NEG-Q and NEG-V deep structures. B. Semantic rules must assign appropriate scope to the NEG and the quantifier "all," so that the NEG-V deep structure is mapped into the NEG-V reading and the NEG-Q deep struc-

---

[8] The actual dialect situation is complicated; see Chapters 3 and 4. The dialect I describe in this chapter is one of the two most common, and includes dialects W, X, and Y_1 of Figure 4.1 (19 informants). For discussion of the relatively uncommon dialects in which (11a) has both NEG-Q and NEG-V readings (Y_2 and Z in Figure 4.1, 5 informants), see especially section 4 of Chapter 4. I know of no informants for whom (11a) has only a NEG-V reading.

ture is mapped into the NEG-Q reading. C. Syntactic rules must map the NEG-Q deep structure into the surface structures of (10 a) and (10 b), and must map the NEG-V deep structure into the surface structure of (10 b).

3.3   Quantifiers under *Not*-Transportation: an Asymmetry

Under standard analyses, a sentence like (11 a) would be derived from the structure Fig. 1 embedded under the /+NT/ verb "think."

   (11) a. John doesn't think that all the boys will run.
          b. John thinks that not all the boys will run. (NEG-Q Reading)
          c. John thinks that all the boys (won't run). (NEG-V Reading)

Such an analysis makes the implicit prediction that (11 a) will share the ambiguity of (10 b). In fact, however, (11 a) has a NEG-Q reading synonymous with (11 b), but no reading synonymous with the NEG-V reading of (11 c).[9] There is thus an asymmetry to account for: any successful analysis must show why (11 a) has only a NEG-Q reading when (10 b) has both a NEG-Q and NEG-V reading.

In the meaning-preserving analysis we are developing, we proposed to account for the ambiguity of (10 b) by deriving it from distinct NEG-Q and NEG-V deep structures. To account simultaneously for the unambiguity of (11 a), we must show that the NEG in the NEG-Q structure is available for NT, but that the NEG in the NEG-V structure is not.

3.4   Possible Solutions

Our approach will be to propose analyses that handle the ambiguity of (10 b), and to test these analyses against (11 a) and other sentences. The first step, therefore, is to modify the base component to produce distinct NEG-Q and NEG-V deep structures. There are two basic ways to go about this:

I. We could complicate the analysis of negation by dividing the functions of Klima's sentence negation between two new negatives, one semantically interpreted as NEG-Q and the other semantically interpreted as NEG-V.

II. We could complicate the deep structure of quantifiers, so that there were

---

[9] In an earlier version of this argument (Carden 1968a), I described the NEG-V reading of (11a) as synonymous with (F1):

  (F1) John thinks that none of the boys will run.

While this is of course true, it caused some confusion, since it was possible (Jackendoff 1968b, 1971) to imagine that I intended to claim that (11c) had the same deep structure as (F1). It is not necessary to the argument that (11c) and (F1) have the same deep structure, though of course it is possible that they might.

two places where the same sentence-negation base rule could apply; the resulting deep structure would be semantically interpreted as NEG-Q if the NEG was inserted at one location, and as NEG-V if the NEG was inserted at the other.

In the following sections I argue that the second approach is correct: we need a new deep structure for quantifiers.

3.4.1 Possible Solution I: Change Negation

Solution I a: Quantifier Negation

Given the hypothesis that a quantifier is a deep-structure constituent of the NP it modifies, one natural move is to define a "quantifier negation" by a base rule of the form "Quantifier → (NEG) *all*." Semantic rules would then interpret the quantifier negation as the NEG-Q reading and the original sentence negation as the NEG-V reading.

Fig. 2

Quantifier-Negation Deep Structures for (10 a b)

a. NEG-Q Deep Structure (quantifier negation)

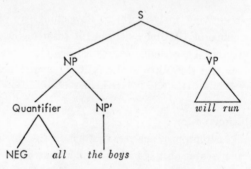

b. NEG-V Deep Structure (sentence negation)

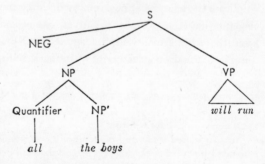

This analysis has two flaws:

1.   Some special mechanism will be needed to distinguish the new quantifier negation, which is a sentence negation by Klima's tests, from Klima's constituent negation, which is not.

2.   The structures in Fig. 2 implicitly make a prediction about the behavior of negated quantifiers under *Not*-Transportation: The NEG attached to S in Fig. 2 b should move under NT like any other sentence negation, while the NEG buried under "Quantifier" in Fig. 2 a should not be affected by NT. That is, these structures predict that (11 a) will have a NEG-V reading, but no NEG-Q reading. This is the reverse of the observed facts, and the analysis must therefore be rejected.

Solution 1 b: VP Negation

Suppose we reverse the analysis in Fig. 2, and replace the quantifier-negation base rule with one that inserts a "VP-Negation":

Fig. 3
VP-Negation Deep Structures for (10 a b)

a.   NEG-Q Deep Structure: NEG-on-S

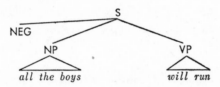

b.   NEG-V Deep Structure: VP Negation

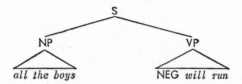

We should then need a syntactic rule or rules, roughly equivalent to Klima's, saying that NEG-on-S optionally appears on the quantifier if one is present, and otherwise on the main verb. A rule of semantic interpretation would also be needed to perform substantially the same operation, with the difference that NEG-on-S is obligatorily interpreted as NEG-Q if a quantifier is present. A second semantic rule would interpret VP-Negation as NEG-V. Assuming that the independently-motivated statement of NT would apply only to NEG-on-S, this analysis will produce the right surface structures and meanings for (11 a).

There are, however, some problems:

1.   A sentence with a negative and no quantifier will have two deep structures

even though the sentence is not ambiguous.

2. The syntactic rule(s) that move NEG-on-S into its surface position and the semantic rule(s) that interpret NEG-on-S perform essentially the same operation—associating NEG-on-S with the quantifier. The analysis is therefore redundant.

3. Regardless of the relative order of Passive and NEG-Placement, the active-passive relation will not work in a sentence with two quantifiers:

> (12)   a.   ACTIVE: Not many boys hit all the balls.
>
>   b.   PASSIVE before NEG-Placement:
>   Not all the balls were hit by many boys.
>
>   c.   ACTIVE: Not many boys didn't hit all the balls.
>
>   d.   NEG-Placement before PASSIVE:
>   *All the balls weren't hit by not many boys.

(12a) and (12b) are not synonymous, and (12d) is starred. If we move the offending "not" away from "many," we get (12e), which is even worse:

> (12)   e.   *All the balls weren't not hit by many boys.

The problem is that we need to be able to put a NEG on either quantifier independently, which under the proposed system would require one S per quantifier.[10]

3.4.2 Possible Solution II: Quantifiers from a Higher Sentence

Suppose we did have one S per quantifier. Recall the generalization stated in section 3.1: NT takes a negative only from the topmost S embedded under a /+NT/ verb. Notice further that the meaning pattern in (11) is parallel to that in (9). If a quantifier sentence like (13) has a deep structure in which the quantifier "all" appears in a higher S than the main verb "will run," then we can explain the meaning pattern of (11) by the same generalization that governed the meaning of (9).

---

[10] This is a variation of the scope problem discussed in Chapter 5. The VP-Negation solution could be extended to handle (12) by using surface-structure semantic-interpretation rules (Jackendoff 1969b) or equivalent derivational constraints, but these would still be unable to handle (14ab).

(13)   All the boys will run.

Fig. 4

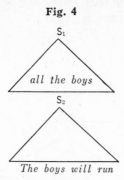

The boys will run

Consider what happens when a structure like Fig. 4 is negated. The existing base rule for sentence negation will attach a NEG either to S_1 or to S_2. If a NEG is attached to S_1, the existing semantic rules will interpret it as applying to S_1, giving the NEG-Q reading. If a NEG is attached to S_2, the same rules will interpret it as applying only to S_2, giving the NEG-V reading. If quantifiers come from a deep structure like Fig. 4, therefore, we can account for the ambiguity of (10 b) with no complication of the base and semantic rules affecting negation.[11]

In this analysis, the sentences in (11) would be derived from a negated Fig. 4 embedded under "John thinks":

[11] The derivation requires NEG-Placement and Quantifier-Lowering rules (see section 4.2 of this chapter) and a Quantifier-NEG-Moving rule (see Carden 1968a).

NEG-Q Deep Structure: Starting with a NEG on S_1, NEG-Placement attaches the NEG to *all*. Quantifier-Lowering attaches *all* and its NEG to the NP *the boys*. This gives (10a). Quantifier-NEG-Moving optionally moves the NEG from *all* onto the main verb, giving (10b).

NEG-V Deep Structure: Starting with a NEG on S_2, NEG-Placement attaches the NEG to *will run*. Quantifier-Lowering attaches *all* to *the boys*, giving (10b).

Fig. 5
Higher-S Deep Structure for (11 a b c)

a. NEG-Q Deep Structure

    (11 b)   John thinks that not all the boys will run.

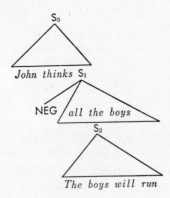

b. NEG-V Deep Structure

    (11 c)   John thinks that all the boys (won't run).

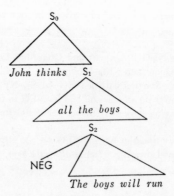

The existing NEG-Placement rules will produce the surface structure (11 b) from Fig. 5 a and the NEG-V reading of (11 c) from Fig. 5 b.[12] What about (11 a)?

---

[12] It is interesting and unexplained that some informants who find (10b) has both NEG-Q and NEG-V readings find that (11c) has only a NEG-V reading, so that (11c) is disambiguated in the opposite direction to (11a). A clearly related observation is that some informants who find that (10b) has only the NEG-Q reading find that (11c) has a (sometimes ungrammatical) NEG-V reading.

(11 a)   John doesn't think that all the boys will run.

(11 a) is derived when *Not*-Transportation moves a NEG from the embedded S onto the $/+NT/$ verb "think." By the generalization stated in section 3.1, a NEG in S_1 can be moved by NT, but a NEG in S_2 cannot. The analysis thus correctly predicts that (11 a) will have a NEG-Q reading, but no NEG-V reading.

The higher-S analysis of quantifiers (Fig. 4) thus accounts for both the ambiguity of (10 b) and the unambiguity of (11 a) with no complication in the analyses of negation and *Not*-Transportation. The price we pay is a major complication in the analysis of quantifiers. Two steps are necessary before we can accept this complication: 1. We must discover the internal structure of the mysterious higher sentence. 2. We must find independent motivation for the higher sentence.

3.5   Side Excursion: The NT Argument in a More Powerful Model

The *Not*-Transportation argument presented in the preceding sections depends on the hypothesis that syntax is meaning preserving. It is interesting to ask whether the argument would collapse if we adopted a more powerful model for language.

Consider, for example, the analyses of quantifiers and negation in Jackendoff (1969b) and G. Lakoff (1969). These analyses determine relative scope—the difference between our NEG-Q and NEG-V readings—using surface-structure semantic-interpretation rules (Jackendoff) or derivational constraints (Lakoff). Could either analysis handle the NT asymmetry (10b vs. 11a) without the higher-S analysis of quantifiers?

While either analysis could be extended to handle the particular examples we have been talking about (10b, 11a) without using a higher-S deep structure, there are examples for which no such extension is possible:

(14)   a.   The marksman didn't hit all the targets.

NEG-Q Reading: $\sim((\forall x \; \epsilon \; \text{the targets}) \; (\text{hit (the marksman, x)}))$

(He hit some, but not all.)

NEG-V Reading: $(\forall x \; \epsilon \; \text{the targets}) \; (\sim(\text{hit (the marksman, x)}))$

(He missed all the targets.)

b.   The party doesn't expect all its candidates to win.

NEG-Q Reading: The party expects $[\sim((\forall x \; \epsilon \; \text{its candidates}) \; (\text{win} \; (x)))]$

(It expects some to win, but not all.)

NEG-V Reading: The party expects $[(\forall x \; \epsilon$ its candidates) $(\sim($win
$(x)))]$

(It expects all to lose.)

The Jackendoff-Lakoff analyses are based on the hypothesis that relative scope is determined by surface-structure primacy relations; see Chapter 5 for details and discussion. Consider now the dialect[13] in which (14a) is ambiguous between NEG-Q and NEG-V readings, often with stress or intonation disambiguating, but (14b) has only the NEG-Q reading under any stress or intonation. This asymmetry between (14a) and (14b) is the same as that between (10b) and (11a). But the surface-structure primacy relations between NEG and "all" are identical in (14a) and (14b), so no mechanism based on surface-structure primacy relations can account for the difference in readings.

The higher-S analysis, however, accounts for this asymmetry directly: (14a) has a deep structure parallel to Fig. 4, and is ambiguous in the same way as (10b). (14b) is derived by *Not*-Transportation from a deep structure parallel to Fig. 5a, and is unambiguous for the same reason as (11a).[13a]

We can conclude that, in the relevant dialect, the higher-S analysis will be needed independently of the existence of mechanisms permitting relative scope to be determined by surface-structure primacy relations.

4. Internal Structure of the Higher S[14]

First, why do we assume that the higher structure involved is an S rather than some special operator like the logicians' $\forall$? There are three reasons: 1. Simplicity of base: the existing phrase-structure rules generate S. 2. Simplicity of embedding: S already appears in the appropriate complements. 3. Simplicity of *Not*-Transportation: As shown by (9), NT already operates on the highest embedded S.

Further simplicity arguments make it possible to assign some internal structure to the quantifier S. At the least it must contain the quantifier, the sentence that contains the quantifier in surface structure, and some way of determining

---

[13] This dialect is relatively uncommon (5 informants to date), since most informants find that (14a) has only the NEG-Q reading.

[13a] The higher-S analyses in chapters 4 and 5 suggest that the relative scope of *all* and NEG in (14b) is determined by the relative order of NT and QL, while the relative scope in (14a) is determined by derivational constraints mentioning shallow structure. Since these processes are presumably independent, these analyses predict that, as observed, the readings of (14a) will not necessarily parallel those of (14b). See also Appendix B, section 5.2.

[14] George Lakoff suggested the line of argument followed in this section.

which NP in that S is modified by the quantifier. The natural way to indicate which NP is the quantified one is to put a copy of it into the quantifier S: this S will then contain Q, S, and NP.

4.1 Relative Clause Structure

Since the NP in the quantifier S determines which NP in the lower S is modified by the quantifier, we must make sure we don't generate structures where the NP in the quantifier S_1 is not matched by any NP in the embedded S_2. A similar problem arises with relative clauses since, in any restrictive-relative clause structure like (15), S_2 must contain a copy of NP_1:

(15)

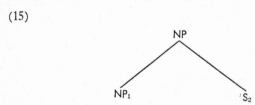

If we combine our S and NP into a restrictive-relative structure (15), we shall be able to use the same mechanism to solve both problems.

Is there any evidence that quantifiers do in fact have a restrictive-relative deep structure? First, some quantifiers can appear, with varying acceptability according to dialect, in surface structures parallel to (15). For example, (16a) and (16b) are synonymous:

(16)   a.   The boys who left were many.
        b.   Many of the boys left.

Second, the pre-suppositions of sentences with restrictive-relative clauses and of sentences with quantifiers are the same. For example, (17a) and (17b) both have deep structures with S_2 a restrictive relative embedded in S_1:

(17)   a.   I deny that the boys who left ran. (restrictive relative)

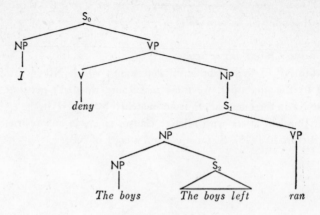

b.   I deny that all the boys left. (Quantifier)

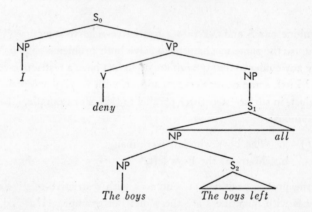

In (a) the speaker denies that the boys ran (S_1) but asserts that they left (S_2); we therefore predict that in (b) the speaker will deny S_1 and assert S_2. This is the case: the speaker asserts that boys left (S_2) but denies that the boys who left were all the boys (S_1). The structure shown in (15) is thus indirectly confirmed.

4.2   Quantifiers as Verbs:

If we adopt the restrictive-relative structure of (15), the complete tree for a sample sentence will look something like this:

(18)   All the boys left.

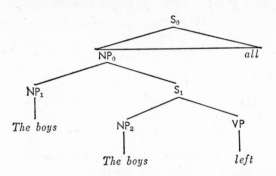

The top sentence S_0 then consists of NP_0 and the quantifier "all." Such a structure is generated by the existing base rules only if the quantifier is a form of verb.
There is some further evidence to support making the quantifier a verb:

1.   Placement of NEG: In ordinary sentences the NEG usually appears
on the verb; in a deep structure like (18) a NEG on S_0 would normally appear
on the quantifier. If the quantifier is the verb of S_0 then the same rule will serve
to attach NEGs to either quantifiers or ordinary verbs.

2.   Adjective parallels: In the next chapter I shall give evidence that quantifiers in phrases of the form "the many men who . . ." should be described as
verbs of non-restrictive relative clauses, an extension of the usual analysis
(Smith (1961 and 1964) and Ross (1966)) for attributive, pre-nominal adjectives.
If this proposal is correct, and the "many" in (19) is a verb, then there is plainly
an economy in analyzing the homonymous and synonymous quantifier in (20)
as a verb as well.

(19)   The many men who voted for McCarthy were disappointed.

(20)   I don't think many boys left.

3.   The quantifier appears overtly as the predicate in examples like (16a).

If we do analyze the quantifier as a verb, we get this tree for (18):

(18)   All the boys left

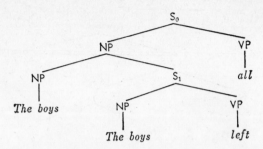

We shall now need a magical rule to transform this structure into a reasonable surface structure. Such a rule might look like this:

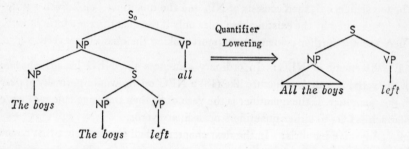

If we order this Quantifier Lowering rule (QL) after *Not*-Transportation, we can get the correct surface structures for (11) from semantically plausible deep structures using the existing NT rule:

(11 a and b)   John thinks that not all the boys will run.

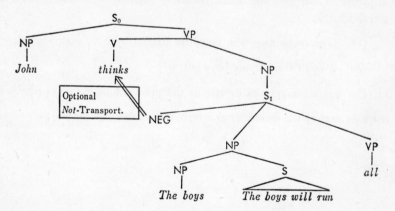

(11 c)   John thinks that all the boys (won't run).

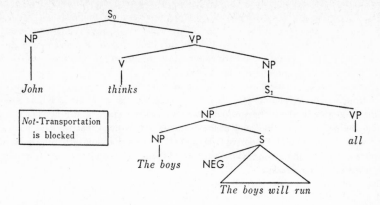

5. Independent Motivation

A structure of the sort developed in section 4 will help to explain presuppositions in quantifier sentences (4.1) and the appearance of negatives on quantifiers (4.2). It also avoids the Active-Passive Problem of (12), since a special rule of NEG-Placement for quantifiers is not needed.[15] Still, the primary justification for the analysis is that it is the simplest available explanation for the *Not*-Transportation meaning patterns in (11).

This is scanty evidence for a change as important as that proposed.[16] Much

[15] Two quantifiers would require two higher Ss and admit, potentially, two NEGs. Plainly controlling recursion will be a problem. See also the discussion of the scope problem in Chapter 5.

[16] If other rules in which a higher S disappears turn out to be needed to explain auxiliaries, adverbs, or prepositions, the plausibility of Quantifier Lowering should be increased. Compare Lakoff (1965 section F) and Ross (1967).

There is a continuing controversy on the status of quantifiers in deep or underlying structure. Lakoff (1965), (1969), (1970a), and I (1967), (1968a) argue on essentially independent grounds that quantifiers appear in underlying structure as the predicates of higher sentences. Our respective positions are attacked by Partee (1970) and Jackendoff (1968a, b, 1971). Ross (1968), without committing himself to the higher-S analysis, sketches an additional argument for it.

Some of the points at issue are:

1.   The higher-S analysis requires an as-yet-unspecified rule of Quantifier Lowering (QL) to move the quantifier from the higher-S down to its surface-structure position. Since I have made no proposal for the derived-structure output of QL, it is reasonable for Jackendoff to complain (1968a, 14) that the higher-S analysis ignores the "more obvious aspects" of quantifiers. It appears that the facts about quantifiers fall into two natural classes: (1) The more obvious, surface-structure facts, which can be explained by an analysis using

some structure A, possibly similar to the one proposed by Jackendoff. (2) Deeper, more "semantic" facts which can be explained by a higher-S analysis similar to the one Lakoff and I propose. Moreover, it appears that all the rules requiring the higher-S structure precede the rules requiring structure A. I claim, therefore, that there is no conflict between these analyses: if we make A the derived-structure output of QL, we shall have a combined analysis that explains both sets of facts.

2. Jackendoff points out that my analysis of the interaction of quantifiers and negation differs from that in Klima (1964b). That is necessarily the case: since Klima was not working in a system where transformations preserved meaning, he did not need to distinguish the negated-quantifier and negated-main-verb readings that we have been concerned with. He could and did derive (10a) and (10b) from the same structure. Jackendoff continues and shows that, using Klima's rules, (11a) and (11') can be derived from semantically plausible deep structures:

(11a)   John doesn't think that all the boys will run.

(11')   John thinks that none of the boys will run.

The difficulty, not noticed by Jackendoff, arises with (11b) and (11c). If Klima's NEG-Incorporation-into-Indefinites rule is obligatory, you cannot get (11c) at all, while if it is optional you get (11a), (11b), and (11c) from the same structure. Since (11c) does not share any readings with (11a) and (11b), this is a fatal flaw in any system that requires transformations to preserve meaning. This particular problem could be solved without a higher sentence by making "verb negation" distinct from "quantifier negation" as in section 3.4, but then other problems appear.

3.   Jackendoff points out (1968b p. 58) that the Equi-NP-Deletion argument for the higher-S analysis (Carden 1968a) can be reconstructed for generics. He concludes from this "The problem, then, is probably not one of finding a new derivation for quantifiers, but rather one of formulating "coreferentiality" in such a way as to explain the interpretation of plural and generic noun phrases in these complement constructions." I agree with the observation about generics (first brought to my attention by Richard Miller), but would conclude from it that generics and quantifiers, which form a semantic class, also form a syntactic class and share a higher-verb deep structure.

of the rest of the book will be devoted to developing additional evidence for the higher-S hypothesis proposed in this chapter; at this point I shall limit myself to pointing out that the higher-S analysis offers at least an approach to the anaphora problems outlined in section 2.

Consider a higher-S deep structure for (la):

(la) Every optimist$_i$ expects every optimist$_i$ to be President.

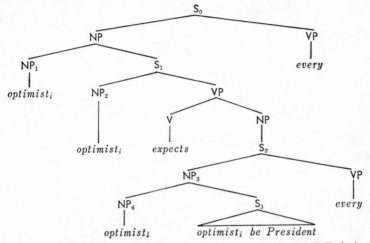

At this stage NP$_2$ is not equal to NP$_3$, so there is no way Equi-NP Deletion can apply. If Equi-NP Deletion is ordered so that it applies before QL, there will be no problem with (la) reducing to (lb).

(lb), on the other hand, will have a deep structure like this:

(lb) Every optimist expects to be President.

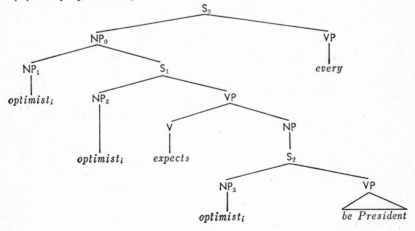

If Equi-NP Deletion applies before QL, as we saw was required for (la), NP_2 and NP_3 will be equal, so that (lb) will reduce to (21):

(21)

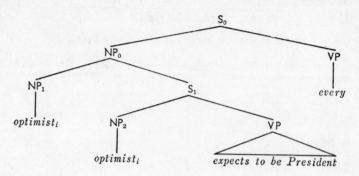

QL will then give the desired result (22):

(22)

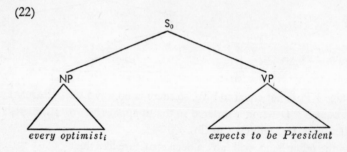

Chapter 2:

The Underlying Structure of Post-Determiner Quantifiers[1]

1. Introduction

Words of the class known as quantifiers appear in English in three surface-structure positions:

A. Pre-Determiner
 a) All (of) the boys   b) Many (of the) boys
B. Post-Determiner[2]
 a) *The all boys   b) The many boys
C. Overt Predicate[2]
 a) *The boys were all.   b) The boys were many.

[1] This chapter is a slightly revised verion of "On Post-Determiner Quantifiers," originally published in *Linguistic Inquiry* 1:415–27 (1970).

 Several of my example sentences are derivative: Examples IX and XV from Partee (1970), Example XIII and its interpretation from G. Lakoff (1970a), and the Pre-Determiner sentences of the following examples: IV from Ross (1968), VI from Lakoff and Bach, VII from Lees via Lakoff (1965), X from Lakoff, and XII from Perlmutter. I also wish to acknowledge helpful advice from George Lakoff and David Perlmutter, who read earlier versions of this chapter. I should make it clear that the people who have advised me or whose examples I have used do not necessarily agree with anything I say.

 The analysis I give here was proposed on essentially independent grounds in Carden (1967) and Lakoff (1970a). Lakoff, using Partee's observation that Overt-Predicate quantifiers do not appear in restrictive relatives, was the first to show the non-restrictive nature of Post-Determiner quantifiers.

[2] I have not indicated any distinction in acceptability between archaic-sounding constructions like (Cb) and fully grammatical sentences. Also, I have used Post-Determiner quantifiers freely without a following relative clause. These conventions are not important to any of the arguments, and the reader should add relative clauses and /+Archaic-sounding/

Most effort has been spent on the Pre-Determiner Quantifiers (Q), which are rightly thought to show the most interesting and quantifier-like behavior. The Post-Determiner Q, when they have been mentioned at all, have apparently been assumed to be syntactically closely related to the Pre-Determiner Q.[3] The Overt-Predicate Q are either ungrammatical or archaic-sounding for most Q.

In this chapter I am concerned with the relation of these three quantifier structures and, in particular, with the deep structure underlying the Post-Determiner Q surface structure. It seems clear that the difference between the structures is not determined lexically, i.e. that "many" is the same lexical item in A, B, and C. The different surface structures, therefore, must come from different deep structures; or, if two come from the deep structure, one must have undergone some optional rule.

It is helpful to consider first what we know about Pre-Determiner Q. Superficially, quantifiers resemble adjectives: they appear with and modify nouns. Pre-Determiner Q, however, differ in surface structure from true adjectives. As we saw in Chapter 1, they also differ from the adjectives in "deeper" ways, and authors have proposed a wide range of underlying structures to account for the observed peculiarities.[4] In this chapter I give twelve constructions in which Pre-Determiner Q differ syntactically or semantically from the adjectives.

Turning to Post-Determiner Q, we notice first that they have a surface structure like that of true adjectives. More significantly, in the twelve cases where Pre-Determiner Q acted unlike true adjectives, the Post-Determiner Q act like the adjectives and unlike the Pre-Determiner Q. When we examine two additional constructions, we find that Post-Determiner Q act specifically like non-restrictive adjectives.

This suggests, of course, that Post-Determiner Q should be derived from a deep structure analogous to that of non-restrictive adjectives. The usual analysis[5] of non-restrictive adjectives derives them from non-restrictive relative clauses, thus:

(1)   The Chinese, who are industrious ⇒ The industrious Chinese

A parallel analysis for Post-Determiner Q would derive them from Overt-Predicate Q in non-restrictive relative clauses:

(2)   The boys, who were many ⇒ The many boys

----

markers as required by his dialect.
[3] See, for example, Partee (1970).
[4] Jackendoff (1968a) gives a useful summary of recent proposals.
[5] Originally by Carlota Smith (1961 and 1964).

This analysis is confirmed by two additional pieces of evidence:

A.   The same quantifiers ("many," etc.) that are acceptable (though archaic-sounding) in the Overt-Predicate position also appear in Post-Determiner position. The ones ("all," etc.) that are ungrammatical in Over-Predicate position are also ungrammatical in Post-Determiner position. If the Post-Determiner Q are derived from Overt-Predicate Q, this follows automatically.

B.   1) Post-Determiner Q are never interpreted as restrictive; 2) Overt-Predicate Q are ungrammatical in restrictive relative clauses. If the Post-Determiner Q are derived from Overt-Predicate Q, 1 follows automatically from 2.

The first part of the chapter consists of examples supporting the argument above. Examples I through XII show constructions in which Post-Determiner Q act like true adjectives and unlike Pre-Determiner Q. Examples XIII and XIV show constructions where the Post-Determiner Q are demonstrably non-restrictive, and Example XV shows that Overt-Predicate Q do not appear in restrictive relative clauses.

In the conclusion, I outline the way the analysis of Post-Determiner and Overt-Predicate quantifiers proposed here can be combined with the analysis of Pre-Determiner quantifiers proposed in Chapter 1, resulting in a unified analysis of quantifiers in all three surface-structure positions.

2.   True Adjectives, Pre-Determiner Q, and Post-Determiner Q

2.1   Examples Involving Negation

I.   *Not*-Transportation

With certain *Not*-Transportation (NT) verbs we find an interesting pattern of synonymy between sentences with a surface-structure negative (NEG) on the NT verb and similar sentences with a NEG in a complement sentence. Various transformational and interpretive rules have been proposed to explain these patterns,[6] but at this point we are concerned with the patterns themselves, not with any particular explanation of them.

Consider first the pattern for sentences with a true adjective in the complement S.

(3)   a.   John doesn't think the attractive girls left.
      b.   John thinks the attractive girls stayed. (NEG "leave")
      c.   John thinks the unattractive girls left. (NEG "attractive")

(3a), the sentence with the negative NT verb, has a reading synonymous with

[6] See Chapter 1, footnote 7 (p. 16).

(3b), the sentence with the main verb of the complement S negated. (3a), however, has no reading synonymous with (3c), the sentence with a true adjective in the complement S negated. Schematically:

NEG NT verb = NEG main verb in comp S

NEG NT verb ≒ NEG true adjective in comp S

As we saw in Chapter 1, a different pattern appears with Pre-Determiner Q:

(4) a. John doesn't think that all the girls left.
     b. John thinks that all the girls stayed. (NEG "leave")
     c. John thinks that not all the girls left. (NEG "all")

Here (4a), with the negative NT verb, has a reading synonymous with (4c), the sentence with the negated Pre-Determiner Q. But (4a) has no reading synonymous with (4b), the sentence with the main verb of the complement S negated. Schematically:

NEG NT verb ≒ NEG main verb in comp S

NEG NT verb = NEG Pre-Determiner Q in comp S

This pattern is just the opposite of the one found for true adjectives; and we have seen that there will be problems explaining both by the same rule, unless Pre-Determiner Q have a structure markedly different from that of true adjectives.

No such problem arises with Post-Determiner Q, which conform exactly to the true adjective pattern:

(5) a. John doesn't think the many girls left.
     b. John thinks the many girls stayed. (NEG "leave")
     c. John thinks the few girls left. (NEG "many")

Here (5a) has a reading synonymous with (5b), but no reading synonymous with (5c). Schematically:

NEG NT verb = NEG main verb in comp S

NEG NT verb ≒ NEG Post-Determiner Q in comp S

II. "Deny"

Similar, and presumably related, patterns appear with sentences embedded under "deny":

(6) a. John denies the Whig candidates won.

                    Assumes there were Whig candidates.

. Denies that they won.

b.   John denies that many candidates won.

Assumes there were candidates who won.
Denies that they were many.

c.   John denies that the many candidates won.

Assumes that there were many candidates.
Denies that they won.

Here, as with *Not*-Transportation, Post-Determiner Q and true adjectives work one way, and Pre-Determiner Q work another.

III.   Overt Negatives

An overt negative ("not") cannot modify a pre-nomial true adjective, though an absorbed negative ("un-", "dis-", etc.) is grammatical:
Overt:

(7)   a.   *The not happy inmates escaped.
      b.   *Not happy inmates escaped.

Absorbed:

(8)   a.   The unhappy inmates escaped.
      b.   Unhappy inmates escaped.

Pre-Determiner Q do not follow the true-adjective pattern, but tolerate a preceding overt negative in some cases. In particular, "not many" is grammatical:

(9)   Not many inmates escaped.

Post-Determiner Q, however, follow the adjective pattern strictly: overt negatives are ungrammatical and absorbed negatives are permitted.
Overt:

(10)   a.   *The not many inmates escaped.
       b.   *Not the many inmates escaped.

Absorbed:

(11)   The few inmates escaped.

IV.   "Than" Clauses

Negatives appear in "than" clauses only in certain cases. For example, overt and absorbed negatives on the main verb of the clause are blocked:

(12) a. *John is prouder than his friends didn't expect.
      b. *John is prouder than his friends denied.

Absorbed[7] negatives on true adjectives, on the other hand, are permitted:

(13) John is prouder than his unhappy friends expected.

Pre-Determiner Q act like main verbs, and both overt and absorbed negatives are blocked:

(14) a. *John is prouder than not many of his friends expected.
      b. *John is prouder than few of his friends expected.

Post-Determiner Q, however, follow the true-adjective pattern, so that absorbed negatives are grammatical:

(15) John is prouder than his few friends expected.

V. Quantifier NEG Moving (QNM)

(16) a. Many (of the) boys didn't leave.
      b. Not many (of the) boys left.
      c. Many (of the) boys stayed.

In most dialects (16b) is a possible reading of (16a), in some dialects it is the main or only reading.

This synonymy is not found with true adjectives: there are no dialects where (17a) has (17b) as a possible reading.

(17) a. Happy boys didn't leave. ≠
      b. Unhappy boys left.

Similarly, this synonymy is not found with Post-Determiner Q:

(18) a. The many boys didn't leave. ≠
      b. The few boys left.

A NEG on a main verb in surface structure can (in many dialects) be interpreted as modifying a Pre-Determiner Q, but never as modifying a true adjective or a Post-Determiner Q.

2.2 Noun-Phrase Identity Examples
VI. Equi-NP Deletion

Sentences like (19a) are ungrammatical on the reading where both occurences

---

[7] An overt negative is blocked on independent grounds. See Example III.

of "The Whig candidates" are co-referential.[8]

(19) a. *The Whig candidates$_i$ expect the Whig Candidates$_i$ to be elected.
      b. The Whig candidates expect to be elected.

Despite its ungrammaticality, (19a) can be interpreted, and it is synonymous with (19b). Various analyses[9] have been proposed to explain these facts; but here, as before, we are not concerned with any particular analysis. What is important to the present argument is that, in sentences like (19a), where the identical, co-referential noun phrases are modified by a true adjective ("Whig"), the following facts hold: A. The sentence without deletion (19a) is ungrammatical. B. The sentence without deletion (19a) is synonymous with the sentence with deletion (19b).

Sentences where the identical, co-referential noun phrases are modified by Pre-Determiner Q appear to be exceptions: neither fact A nor fact B is true for them:

(20) a. All the candidates$_i$ expect all the candidates$_i$ to be elected.
      b. All the candidates expect to be elected.

(20a) is fully grammatical, and it is not synonymous with (20b). When the identical, co-referential noun phrases are modified by Post-Determiner Q, we return to the adjective pattern:

(21) a. *The many candidates$_i$ expect the many candidates$_i$ to be elected.
      b. The many candidates expect to be elected.

The sentence without deletion (21a) is ungrammatical and also is synonymous to the sentence with deletion (21b).

VII. Reflexivization

A similar pattern appears with sentences involving reflexive pronouns:

(22) a. *The foolish men$_i$ pity the foolish men$_i$.
      b. The foolish men pity themselves.

The sentence without reflexivization (22a) is ungrammatical but interpretable; and it is synonymous with the reflexive sentence (22b).

Again sentences where the identical, co-referential noun phrases are modified

[8] Co-referential nouns are indicated by subscripts.
[9] See Postal (1970) for a recent discussion of this problem.

by Pre-Determiner Q appear to be exceptions:

(23) a. All the men$_i$ pity all the men$_i$.
      b. All the men pity themselves.

The sentence without reflexivization (23a) is fully grammatical, but not synonymous to the reflexive sentence (23b).

Sentences with Post-Determiner Q return to the true-adjective pattern of (22):

(24) a. *The many men$_i$ pity the many men$_i$.
      b. The many men pity themselves.

(24a) is ungrammatical, but synonymous with (24b).

VIII. Comparatives

Proposed analyses[10] for the comparative construction have usually depended on repeated identical noun phrases, so that a deep or intermediate structure like (25a) was mapped onto a surface structure like (25b).

(25) a. The west coast cities$_i$ are more far from New York than the west coast cities$_i$ are from Chicago. $\xrightarrow{\text{obligatorily}}$
      b. The west-coast cities$_i$ are farther from New York than from Chicago.

It is an essential feature of such analyses that the deep or intermediate structure (25a) mean the same as the surface structure (25b).

With true adjectives, as in (25), this is no problem; but Pre-Determiner Q show a different pattern:

(26) a. Many (of the) cities$_i$ are more far from New York than many (of the) cities$_i$ are far from Chicago. $\neq$
      b. Many (of the) cities$_i$ are farther from New York than from Chicago.
(27) a. Every city$_i$ is more far from New York than every city$_i$ is far from Chicago. $\neq$
      b. Every city$_i$ is farther from New York than from Chicago.

The (a) sentences above do not mean the same as the (b) sentences, and therefore cannot serve as deep or intermediate structures for them.

This whole problem does not arise for Post-Determiner Q, which repeat the pattern of the true adjectives:

[10] See, for example, Lees (1961) and Lakoff (1965); but compare Ross and Perlmutter (1970) and R. Lakoff (1970).

(28)   a.   The many cities$_1$ are more far from New York than the many

cities$_1$ are far from Chicago. $\xrightarrow[\hspace{3cm}]{\text{obligatorily}}$

b.   The many cities are farther from New York than from Chicago.

Here (28a) and (28b) do mean the same thing.

IX.   Conjunction Reduction

Certain conjoined sentences are synonymous to similar simple sentences containing conjoined phrases; for example, (29a), is synonymous with (29b):

(29)   a.   Good rules$_1$ are explicit and good rules$_1$ are easy to read.
b.   Good rules are (both) explicit and easy to read.

As in the previous examples, sentences where the identical noun phrases are modified by Pre-Determiner Q appear to be exceptions:

(30)   a.   Few (of the) rules$_1$ are explicit and few (of the) rules$_1$ are easy to read.
b.   Few (of the) rules are (both) explicit and easy to read.

Here (30a) is not synonymous with (30b).

Post-Determiner Q, however, follow the pattern of the true adjectives in (29);

(31)   a.   The few rules$_1$ are explicit and the few rules$_1$ are easy to read.
b.   The few rules are explicit and easy to read.

Here (31a) and (31b) are synonymous.

2.3   Miscellaneous Examples
X.   Questions

Questions show a meaning pattern similar to that found in the negation examples of V:

(32)   a.   Did the cholera patients survive? (Questions "survive")
b.   Did many patients survive? (Questions "many")
c.   Did the many patients survive? (Questions "survive")

In (32a) and (32c) it is assumed that the patients were many or were suffering from cholera, and questioned whether they survived; while in (32b) it is assumed that there were patients who survived, and questioned whether the ones survived were many. As in example V, true adjectives and Post-Determiner Q act in one way, while Pre-Determiner Q act in another.

XI. Double Quantifiers

Two Pre-Determiner Q cannot modify the same noun phrase, whether or not one has been moved away from the noun phrase:[11]

> (33)　a.　*All many (of the) boys left.
> 　　　b.　*Many (of the) boys all left.
> 　　　c.　*Many (of the) boys have all left.

On the other hand, Pre-Determiner Q can modify noun phrases already modified by true adjectives or by Post-Determiner Q:

> (34)　a.　All the 5th-grade boys left.
> 　　　b.　All the many boys left.

XII. "Begin"

For some speakers a noun phrase modified by a Pre-Determiner Q cannot appear in the context

$$\text{—— begin to } V_p$$

where the V_p is a point-action verb like "arrive" or "explode". For such speakers (35a) and (35b) are therefore ungrammatical:

> (35)　a.　*All the guests began to arrive.
> 　　　b.　*Many guests began to arrive.

True adjectives and Post-Determiner Q, however, are quite grammatical in such constructions, even for the speakers in question:

> (36)　a.　The welcome guests began to arrive.
> 　　　b.　The many guests began to arrive.

3. An Overt-Predicate Deep Structure

Examples I through XII show that Post-Determiner Q act like true adjectives, suggesting that Post-Determiner Q and adjectives share a deep structure. In this section we consider whether the appropriate deep structure is that of restrictive or of non-restrictive adjectives. Examples XIII and XIV show that Post-Determiner Q act semantically and syntactically like non-restrictives. We conclude

---

[11] This does not apply to quantifiers conjoined by "and," of which a number of combinations are grammatical: "Any and all . . .," "Each and every . . ." Constructions of the form "many, indeed most . . ." are also grammatical.

that Post-Determiner Q, like non-restrictive adjectives, are derived from the predicates of deep-structure non-restrictive relative clauses. Example XV confirms this analysis by showing that Overt-Predicate Q never appear in restrictive relative clauses, thus explaining why Post-Determiner Q are always non-restrictive.

XIII.   Indirect Quotation

(37)   a.   John told me that (the) honest royalists in Bayonne were being slandered.
　　　 b.   (The) royalists in Bayonne are being slandered.
　　　 c.   (The) honest royalists in Bayonne are being slandered.

(37a) shows a particular ambiguity: John may have said (37b), in which case "honest" is the speaker's description of the royalists; or John may have said (37c), in which case "honest" is John's description which the speaker merely reports. It is known[12] that the case in which "honest" is the speaker's description corresponds to (38), where "honest" is introduced in a non-restrictive relative clause.

(38)   John told me that (the) royalists in Bayonne, who are honest, were being slandered.

Indirect quotations with Pre-Determiner Q show this same ambiguity:

(39)   John told me that many (of the) royalists in Bayonne were being slandered.

"Many" can come on John's authority, where the speaker merely reports that John said "Many (of the) royalists in Bayonne are being slandered"; or it may come on the speaker's authority, as where John said (37b) and the speaker describes the royalists as "many."

With Post-Determiner Q, however, no such ambiguity appears:

(40)   John told me that the many royalists in Bayonne were being slandered.

Regardless of John's exact words, the speaker in (40) accepts responsibility for the claim that there are many royalists in Bayonne. If John actually said "The many royalists in Bayonne are being slandered," and the speaker wishes to dissociate himself from the "many," he must use direct quotation or adopt a more elaborate paraphrase like "John told me that the royalists in Bayonne were be-

[12] See Lakoff (1970a).

ing slandered, and he claimed that there were many of them, too."

Post-Determiner Q, in other words, are interpreted only as non-restrictives, so that (40) is synonymous with (41):

> (41) John told me that the royalists in Bayonne, who are many, were being slandered.

This supports the proposed analysis, in which (40) would be derived from (41).

XIV.   ". . . happen to all of them."

Certain constructions, for example (42), seem to require a restrictive relative or its equivalent. (Note that (42b) would be ungrammatical on a non-restrictive reading synonymous with (42d).)

> (42) a. *The students flunked, but it could never happen to all of them.
>   b. The unlucky students flunked, but . . .
>   c. The students who were unlucky flunked, but . . .
>   d. *The students, who were unlucky, flunked, but . . .

Some of the Pre-Determiner Q are grammatical in such constructions:

> (43) Many students flunked, but it could never happen to all of them.

The corresponding Post-Determiner Q, however, are all ungrammatical:

> (44) *The many students flunked, but it could never happen to all of them.

Here we see that, as in the previous examples, Post-Determiner Q act unlike the corresponding Pre-Determiner Q and like true adjectives. However, in this case they do not act like all true adjectives, but only like those that are interpreted as non-restrictive. This gives evidence for the analysis that Post-Determiner Q come from the same deep structure as non-restrictive adjectives.

XV.   Overt-Predicate Parallels

Quantifiers in the Overt-Predicate surface structure can appear only in non-restrictive relative clauses:

> (45) a. The cowards, who were many, ran.
>   b. *The cowards who were many ran.

Given the proposed analysis of Post-Determiner Q as derived from Overt-Predicate Q in relative clauses, we then have an explanation for the facts in XIII and XIV: since the deep-structure source of Post-Determiner Q is necessarily a non-restrictive relative, it follows that Post-Determiner Q will have only the properties of adjectives derived from non-restrictive relatives.

If instead we tried to generate Post-Determiner Q directly in post-determiner position, we should have to state separately, in some unknown way, that they had the same syntactic and semantic properties as adjectives derived from non-restrictive relatives.

4. Conclusion

In examples I through XII we see that Post-Determiner quantifiers act like true adjectives and unlike Pre-Determiner quantifiers: syntactically, Post-Determiner Q are more closely related to true adjectives than to Pre-Determiner Q. Examples XIII and XIV show that Post-Determiner Q act syntactically and semantically as non-restrictives. The proposed analysis explains these facts by deriving Post-Determiner Q from the same deep structure as non-restrictive adjectives, while Pre-Determiner Q are derived from some different deep structure, here unspecified. Adopting the usual analysis of non-restrictive adjectives as deep-structure non-restrictive relative clauses, we conclude that Post-Determiner Q come from a deep-structure non-restrictive relative clause with the quantifier in Overt-Predicate position.

This analysis is confirmed by Example XV, which shows that Overt-Predicate Q never appear in restrictive relatives. It is therefore unnecessary to state that Post-Determiner Q are derived from non-restrictive relatives; by using the Overt-Predicate deep structure motivated by the true-adjective parallels, we ensure that Post-Determiner Q will never be interpreted as restrictive. Additional confirmation comes from the observation that the same set of quantifiers appears in Overt-Predicate and Post-Determiner positions: this follows automatically from our analysis, in which both have the same deep structure.

In this chapter I have concentrated on the similarities between Post-Determiner Q and true adjectives without offering any specific analyses of the constructions involved. My claim is merely that a correct analysis for adjectives, whatever it may be, will also work for Post-Determiner Q.

Likewise, I have shown the differences between Post-Determiner and Pre-Determiner Q without referring to any specific analysis of Pre-Determiner Q. The analysis given here for Post-Determiner Q can, however, be combined with the higher-S analysis of Pre-Determiner Q given in Chapter 1 to form a unified analysis of quantifiers in all three surface-structure positions. This unified analysis goes as follows:

a. The Overt-Predicate structure is basic; i.e., quantifiers appear in deep structure only as predicates.

b.   The Post-Determiner surface structure is generated from an Overt-Predicate Q in a non-restrictive relative clause, using the same rules that apply to true adjectives.

c.   The Pre-Determiner surface structure is generated from an Overt-Predicate Q in a higher sentence, i.e., a sentence dominating the sentence in which the quantifier appears in surface structure. The quantifier is moved down to its surface structure position by a rule of Quantifier Lowering (QL). QL is optional for some quantifiers (e.g., "many"), but the others (e.g., "all") are marked to obligatorily undergo QL, and are thus prevented from appearing in surface structure in Overt-Predicate or Post-Determiner position.

This analysis gives the following pattern:

Pre-Determiner Q:

a.   The boys who left were many. $\xrightarrow{\text{(optional) QL}}$
b.   Many (of the) boys left.

Post-Determiner Q:

a.   The boys, who were many, left. $\xrightarrow{\text{adjective rules}}$
b.   The many boys left.

In other words, I claim that the difference between the Pre-Determiner and Post-Determiner surface structures represents a deep-structure difference in order of embedding, and that the observed syntactic and semantic differences can be predicted from this difference in embedding.

Chapter 3:
Evidence from Idiolect Variation[1]

I. Introduction

Differences among idiolects have long been an embarrassment to transformational grammarians, who regularly find that informants disagree on crucial examples. In some analyses such disagreement seems to imply that the grammars of the conflicting idiolects differ in major structural features, though this unesthetic conclusion is obscured because most analyses describe only one idiolect and mention the others, if at all, as exceptions. In this chapter I wish to argue that there is an obligation to seek an analysis that explains as many as possible of the observed idiolects in a consistent manner, and that a search for a unified analysis can sometimes shed light on difficult theoretical questions.

As an example, I consider sentences involving the interaction of negation, the quantifier *all*, and two polarity-sensitive[2] elements: *until* adverbials and

[1] This chapter is a slightly revised version of "A Note on Conflicting Idiolects," originally published in *Linguistic Inquiry* 1:281–90 (1970).

Susumu Kuno, George Lakoff, and David Perlmutter have read earlier versions of this chapter and given me much good advice and constructive criticism. To them, and to a number of patient informants, I am very grateful. My debt to Edward Klima's work in negation is obvious; the three constructions I use as evidence here were insightfully discussed in Klima (1964b). My mistakes, of course, are my own; and the people who advised me do not necessarily agree with anything I say.

Since writing this chapter I have read Elliott, Legum and Thompson (1969). Using an unrelated example, they make substantially the same point I do: idiolectal variation is part of the relevant data for syntactic analysis, and interesting regularities emerge when such variation is taken into account. They also provide a useful bibliography of papers that use dialectal evidence.
[2] In the sense of Baker (1970b).

positive tag questions. These sentences show superficially confusing and conflicting idiolect partterns of grammaticality and meaning, so that there is a considerable temptation to explain one dialect in an *ad hoc* way and leave the others as exceptions. When we examine the independently motivated constraints on *until* adverbials and tag questions, however, we find that a unified analysis is possible under certain assumptions about rule order and the deep structure of quantifiers. Given these assumptions and a knowledge of the informant's dialect in the simple case (1a), we can predict and explain his responses in the two more complicated cases (2) and (3).

Not by coincidence, the required deep structure for quantifiers turns out to be the higher-S structure for which preliminary motivation was given in Chapter 1. Since this has been a subject of considerable controversy, and individual dialects might be explained under more than one of the competing analyses, it is useful to discover that one analysis offers a unified account of several dialects. The proposed methodology is thus shown to be useful by the very fact that it provides evidence bearing on the controversy about the underlying structure of quantifiers.

2. Quantifier Dialects

(1) a. All the boys didn't leave,
     b. Not all the boys left.
     c. All the boys (didn't leave).

We can distinguish three main dialects for (1a). In one dialect, the negative is always construed with the quantifier, so that (1a) means unambiguously (1b). This I shall call the Negative-Quantifier (NEG-Q) dialect. In the second, the negative is always construed with the verb, so that (1a) unambiguously means (1c), i.e. "All the boys stayed." This I call the Negative-Verb (NEG-V) dialect. In the third, (1a) has both NEG-Q and NEG-V readings. This I call the ambiguous (AMB) dialect.

Taking the three dialects of (1a) as a starting point,[3] let us see what happens when we add polarity-sensitive elements in (2) and (3):

(2) All the boys didn't leave until 6 PM.

---

[3] For the purposes of this chapter I take the dialect pattern of (1a) as given and try to explain the patterns of (2) and (3) consistently with it. The chart in Figure 3.2, showing the permissible deep-structure locations of NEG in the three dialects, is purely descriptive; and at this point I do not try to offer any explanation of the rules or constraints that lead to this pattern. This problem is discussed in Chapter 5.

(3)   All the boys didn't leave, did they?

The chart in Figure 3.1 summarizes the patterns of meaning and grammaticality for the three dialects defined above.

Figure 3.1
Dialect Pattern for Sentences (1a), (2), and (3)[4]

Dialect		Number of informants	Sample Sentence		
			(1a)	(2)	(3)
NEG-Q	A	6	NEG-Q	NEG-V	NEG-Q
	B	10	NEG-Q	*	NEG-Q
NEG-V	A	2	NEG-V	NEG-V	NEG-Q
	B	2	NEG-V	NEG-V	*
AMB	I	13	AMB	NEG-V	NEG-Q
	II	7	AMB	NEG-V	AMB

Total number of informants: 40

Key: NEG-Q indicates the reading in which the NEG is construed with the quantifier, as in (1b); NEG-V indicates the reading in which the NEG is construed with the verb, as in (1c); AMB indicates that the sentence was ambiguous between the NEG-Q and NEG-V readings. * indicates that the sentence was ungrammatical.

[4] Notes to Figure 3.1:

a.   Forty-eight informants were interviewed to get the forty response patterns coded in Figure 3.1. Two were rejected because I could not decide how to code their responses; four because they did not find tag questions grammatical; and two for the reason discussed in (b) below.

b.   As has been noted by Horn (1970) and others, *until* is a bad choice as a test for polarity, since it has two readings that are not polarity sensitive and informants differ on the environments in which the polarity-sensitive reading can appear. The resulting difficulties in coding can be judged from footnotes 5 and 10 in this chapter. In the later interviews (2) was supplemented by (2′), which proved a much more satisfactory test:

(2′)   All the boys didn't budge.

Two informants who were not asked (2′) were coded as accepting a NEG-Q reading for (2); this may be a coding error, or it may be a dialect difference analogous to that between AMB_I and AMB_{II}.

c.   The attention concentrated on the responses to (1a), (2), and (3) should not obscure the fact that other dialectal variations crosscut the ones we are concerned with, so that there are actually a large number of sub-dialects within the NEG-Q, NEG-V, and AMB dialects. A few of these sub-dialects are discussed in the next chapter.

d.   Heringer (1970) reports the results of a questionnaire on sentences parallel to (1a), (2), and (3). Despite the problems associated with the questionnaire methodology, his results seem to agree fairly well with mine: Though his data presentation makes it impossible to deduce the response patterns of all the individual informants, it appears that only seven of his fifty-three informants have dialects differing from those reported here.

To simplify the presentation, in this chapter I shall concentrate on the NEG-Q and NEG-V dialects, and on sub-dialect I within the AMB dialect. In the next chapter I shall take up the relation between sub-dialects I and II and further divisions within the AMB dialect.

Notice that (2) and (3) are not ambiguous in the AMB_I dialect, and that they are disambiguated in opposite directions: (2) with "until" has only a NEG-V reading, while (3) with "did they?" has only a NEG-Q reading. When we look at the NEG-Q and NEG-V dialects, this pattern seems to be confirmed: (2) is ungrammatical in the $NEG-Q_B$ dialect, though all right in the NEG-V dialect; and (3) is all right in the NEG-Q dialect, but ungrammatical in the $NEG-V_B$ dialect. Even more interestingly, the addition of the polarity-sensitive elements causes the speakers of the A sub-dialects to reverse the meaning they got on the simple sentence (la): The speakers of dialect $NEG-Q_A$, who found (la) unambiguously NEG-Q, shift on (2) and find that unambiguously NEG-V. Similarly, the speakers of dialect $NEG-V_A$, who found (la) unambiguously NEG-V, shift on (3) and find that unambiguously NEG-Q. In all cases, "until" favors the NEG-V reading and "did they?" favors the NEG-Q reading.

From only three sentences, then, we have a mass of obviously related but superficially conflicting dialect data. As a first step toward a unified analysis, let us consider the independently-motivated constraints characterizing the cases where "until" and positive ("did they?") tag questions appear.

3. *Until*

Until adverbials can modify non-repetitive readings of point-action predicates like *leave* or *catch the train* only in the presence of a negative:[5]

    (4) a. *John left until 6 PM.
          b. John didn't leave until 6 PM.

Except in cases involving *Not*-Transportation,[6] this negative must appear in the same clause as the *until* adverbial and the point-action predicate:

    (5) a. *The boys who left until 6 PM didn't catch the train.
          b. The boys who didn't leave until 6 PM caught the train.

---

[5] A point-action verb with a plural subject can often be interpreted as indicating an action repeated at short intervals, in which case it occurs freely with *until*:

    F 1) The scouts left until 6 PM, one at a time, slipping off into the dusk . . .

[6] The analysis of *until* sketched here is incomplete but covers the points relevant to the argument.

(6)   a.   *The boys who didn't leave caught the train until 6 PM.
       b.   The boys who left didn't catch the train until 6 PM.

If we represent (5) and (6) by a tree we see that "until" in S_0 (6) requires NEG in S_0, and that "until" in S_1 (5) requires NEG in S_1:

(7)   The boys who left caught the train.

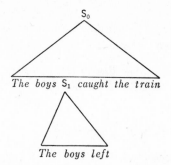

The generalization at this level of analysis is that, whenever "until" and a point-action predicate appear in the same S, that S must be negative in deep structure.

4.   Tag Questions: *did they?*

Among the ways of forming English questions is the Tag-Question rule,[7] which generates sentences like (8ab):

(8)   a.   The boys left, didn't they?
       b.   The boys didn't leave, did they?

While there are various difficulties in stating this rule exactly, two generalizations seem to be well established:

1.   The pro-verb in the tag must be opposite in polarity to the main verb of the questioned sentence: negative "leave" requires positive "do" and vice versa.[8]

(8)   a'.   *The boys left, did they? (as a question)
       b'.   *The boys didn't leave, didn't they?

[7] See Klima (1964b). Examples with performatives present special problems; see R. Lakoff (1969a).
[8] There is a different *did they* tag that is not a question, but seems to mark indignation or challenge: "The students seized the building, did they! We'll soon take care of that." Here we are concerned only with the questioning tag.

2. The form of the tag is based on the topmost non-performative sentence;

(9)   a.   The boys who left were sorry, weren't they?
      b.   *The boys who left were sorry, didn't they?

In particular, a positive tag like "did they?" requires a negative in the topmost non-performative S of the questioned sentence; a negative in an embedded S won't do:

(9)   c.   The boys who left didn't catch the train, did they?
      d.   *The boys who didn't leave caught the train, did they?

With a questioned sentence like that in (7), therefore, a positive *did they?* tag will appear only if S_0 is negative at the time the Tag-Question rule applies.

5.   *Until* and *did they?* with Quantifiers

How can these generalizations about *until* and *did they?* be applied to our problem with quantifier sentences? It turns out that, if we assign these quantifier sentences a deep structure parallel to (7), putting the quantifier in a "higher S," the observed results with (2) and (3) will follow directly from the dialect patterns observed for (la) and the generalizations outlined in sections 3 and 4. Suppose (10) has the deep structure in (10),[9] as proposed in Chapter 1:

(10)   All the boys left.

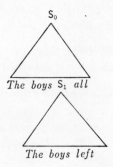

With this structure a negative modifying the quantifier would appear in S_0, corresponding to the NEG-Q reading of (la); and a negative modifying the verb would appear in S_1, corresponding to a NEG-V reading. The permissible loca-

[9] Here I do not specify the internal structure of the higher sentence S_0, since the argument holds regardless of the details of internal structure.

tions for NEG in the three dialects, therefore, are those shown in Figure 3.2.

Figure 3.2

Dialect	Possible Location of NEG	
	NEG S_0	NEG S_1
NEG-Q	×	
NEG-V		×
AMB	×	×

Recalling the generalizations discussed in sections 3 and 4, we can see that adding the polarity-sensitive elements will place additional restrictions on the permissible locations for NEG.

If we add "until 6 PM" to S_1 in (10) then by the *until* constraints S_1 will have to be negative in deep structure, as in the NEG-V reading. A NEG-Q reading, which requires S_0 to be negative in deep structure, should be ungrammatical for the same reason as (5a). Thus the NEG-Q reading of (2) should be ungrammatical in both the NEG-Q and AMB dialects.

As a general rule, when one reading of a potentially ambiguous sentence is ungrammatical, the informant is only aware of the grammatical reading or readings. Only a few informants will say that the ungrammatical reading exists, but that the sentence is ungrammatical with that interpretation. We should therefore expect that, while (2) will be ungrammatical in the unambiguous NEG-Q dialect, in the AMB dialect the NEG-Q reading will disappear completely, and only the grammatical NEG-V reading will appear.[10]

If we add "did they?" to the deep structure in (10) we get the opposite result. By the *did they?* constraint, the topmost sentence will have to be negative at the time the Tag-Question rule applies. If we assume that Tag-Question precedes the Quantifier-Lowering rule, the topmost sentence will be S_0 in (10). Since a negative on S_0 corresponds to a NEG-Q reading, we can predict that (3) will show only a NEG-Q reading. A NEG-V reading, corresponding to a NEG in

[10] For many informants (2) can be interpreted to mean "Not until 6 PM did all the boys leave," i.e. "The last boy left at 6 PM." This reading has a structure analogous to (6b), so that the negative and the *until* appear together with the quantifier in S_0: "The boys who left did not (number) all (the boys) until 6 PM." Since "until" does not modify the positive point-action verb "leave," the constraint is not violated and the sentence is grammatical.

Speakers of this sub-dialect who have the NEG-Q dialect for (la) find that (2) has only this reading; those who have the AMB dialect find that (2) is ambiguous between this reading and the NEG-V reading.

S_1, would be ungrammatical for the same reason as (9d). In the NEG-V dialect, therefore, (3) will be ungrammatical, while in the AMB dialect only the NEG-Q reading will appear.[11]

To summarize:

1.   In the NEG-Q dialect, (3) "did they?" should be grammatical, but (2) "until" should not be.

2.   In the NEG-V dialect, (2) "until" should be grammatical, but (3) "did they?" should not be.

3.   In the AMB dialect, only the NEG-Q reading should be grammatical with "did they?"; and only the NEG-V reading should be grammatical with "until."

Comparing these predictions with the meaning pattern we got for (2) "until" and (3) "did they?", we see that the AMB_I, $NEG-Q_B$, and $NEG-V_B$ dialects fit exactly. In the A sub-dialects, we find additional effects offering further confirmation of our analysis:

In $NEG-Q_A$, speakers who get only the NEG-Q reading for the simple sentence (1a) change to the NEG-V reading when "until 6 PM" is added. In $NEG-V_A$, speakers who get only the NEG-V reading for (1a) change to the NEG-Q reading when "did they?" is added. Notice that these changes are parallel to the disambiguation found in the AMB_I dialect. It appears that the structural pressure of the polarity-sensitive elements is sufficient to force a change in the reading of an unambiguous sentence, as well as to disambiguate an ambiguous sentence.[12]

We can conclude that the higher-S structure of (10), which was supported directly and indirectly by the arguments in Chapters 1 and 2,[13] has the additional advantage of permitting us to describe the dialects of (2) and (3) using the generalizations of sections 3 and 4.

---

[11] One might expect that, in the NEG-V and AMB dialects, sentences like "All the boys didn't leave, didn't they?" would be grammatical on the NEG-V reading. This is true for a few informants, but it appears that late rules restricting double negation block such sentences for most informants. Data and further discussion appear in the next chapter.

[12] These examples, where the addition of context forces a reading that is not present without the context, are bad news for semantic theories like those of Katz and Postal (1964), where additional context can only disambiguate a sentence, never add a new reading. See Carden (1972) for further discusion.

[13] As Example V of Chapter 2 shows, Post-Determiner quantifiers do not display the sort of dialect variation discussed in this chapter. This chapter thus provides additional indirect evidence for the distinction in underlying structure between Pre- and Post-Determiner quantifiers.

6. Conclusion

This chapter began with the claim that we should require an analysis to explain dialect variations in a unified and consistent way, and that by adopting such a principle we gain a useful tool for choosing among competing hypotheses. The rest of the chapter shows the application of this principle to a sample problem, the deep structure of English quantifiers.

The higher-S analysis of quantifiers makes it possible to explain the dialect patterns of (2) and (3), starting from the three dialects of (la) and using independently motivated constraints on *until* and tag questions. In turn, therefore, the dialect patterns of (2) and (3) provide evidence for the higher-S analysis. Moreover, because this analysis handles the dialect data in a unified way, so that the patterns of (2) and (3) follow automatically from the pattern of (la), the proposed principle gives us reason to prefer the higher-S analysis to any competing analysis that describes the different dialects by unrelated rules or *ad hoc* constraints. If the proposed principle is adopted, it then becomes the responsibility of the proponents of alternate analyses of quantifiers to show how their systems would handle the dialect data of (2) and (3) in a unified and consistent way. By comparing the results we can choose among the analyses.

Chapter 4:

Rule Order, Randomness, and Syntactic Dialect Variation[1]

1. Introduction

In the preceding chapter I considered the reactions of a sample of forty informants to sentences like (1), finding NEG-Q, NEG-V, and AMB dialects and various sub-dialects.

(1) All the boys didn't leave.

In this chapter I look at a partially overlapping sample of twenty-five informants who have the AMB dialect for (1), and try to explain the various sub-dialects that appear when the informants are asked other test sentences (Figure 4.1).

An especially interesting feature of these dialect variations, and of those in the preceding chapter, is that they do not appear to be correlated with the social class or geographical origin of the informants. Even when we try to control the informants' background tightly, the same variations appear: of the four family groups (parents and school-age children) included in the sample, none was uniform in their reactions to the test sentences. The type of dialect variation we are dealing with, then, is unusual in that the dialects appear to be randomly distributed among speakers of a given class and region. An eventual goal of our analysis should be to offer an explanation for this random distribution.

It turns out that a number of these dialects can be accounted for by the hypothesis that the speakers of the different sub-dialects have grammars with identical rules but differing rule orders. Thus the AMB_I and AMB_{II} sub-dialects

---

[1] A part of the material in this chapter was pressented at the Linguistic Society of America Annual Meeting, Washington, D.C., 30 December 1970, under the title "Rule order and syntactic idiolect variation."

mentioned in the preceding chapter differ in the relative order of the Tag-Question (Tag-Q) and Quantifier-Lowering (QL) rules, while a second pair of sub-dialects differs in the relative order of the Tag-Q and *Not*-Transportation (NT) rules. These ordering results can be tested, since they implicitly make predictions about the relative order of NT and QL. These predictions turn out to be correct, and the ordering hypothesis is confirmed.

Figure 4.1
Dialect pattern for (1), (2), (7), and (11) in this chapter:[2]

Sample S	Dialect			
	W	X	Y	Z
(1)	AMB	AMB	AMB	AMB
(2)	NEG-Q	NEG-Q	AMB	AMB
(7)	OK	*	OK	*
(11)	NEG-Q	NEG-Q	see note a	AMB
Number of informants	7	8	8	2

Total number of informants: 25

This rule-order analysis of dialect variation is reminiscent of earlier work, e.g. Keyser (1963) and Klima (1964a), where geographical and social dialects were analyzed as differences in rule ordering. With the randomly-distributed dialects that we are concerned with, the ordering analysis is especially plausible, since it offers an approach to an explanation of why the dialects are randomly distributed: The crucial examples determining the relative order of NT, QL, and Tag-Q seem likely to be of low frequency, so that the language learner would lack data to decide which order is appropriate.

[2] Notes to Figure 4.1:
  a.   The 8 speakers of Y divide into sub-dialects on (11): 4 get only the NEG-Q reading (sub-dialect Y_1); 3 get both NEG-Q and NEG-V readings (sub-dialect Y_2); and 1 was not asked the relevant questions to find out.
  b.   Forty-two informants were interviewed to get the sample of 25 presented above. Two were rejected because I could not decide how to code their responses; 1 was rejected because he found that (2), while grammatical, had some third reading distinct from the NEG-Q and NEG-V readings we are discussing; 13 were rejected because they got only a NEG-Q reading for (1); and 1 was rejected because he got only a NEG-V reading for (1). This proportion of AMB, NEG-Q, and NEG-V responses for (1) is not representative, since whenever possible I chose informants known to have the AMB dialect. The sample partly overlaps the sample shown in Figure 3.1.

2.   The Interaction of Quantifier-Lowering with Tag-Question

(2)   All the boys didn't leave, did they?

The AMB_I and AMB_{II} sub-dialects mentioned in Chapter 3 are defined by informant reactions to sentences like (2). In the AMB_I sub-dialect, (2) is not ambiguous, but has only the NEG-Q reading. In the AMB_{II} sub-dialect, (2) is ambiguous between NEG-Q and NEG-V readings. Referring to the data chart in Figure 4.1, we see that fifteen informants have the AMB_I sub-dialect and ten have the AMB_{II}.

In Chapter 3 we saw that sub-dialect AMB_I could be accounted for by ordering Tag-Q before QL, so that a positive tag as in (2) could arise only if the NEG was on the quantifier "all" in underlying structure. Thus the positive *did they?* tag would appear only with a NEG-Q reading, and the non-ambiguity of (2) was explained.

In sub-dialect AMB_{II}, however, (2) remains ambiguous. Suppose that the rule order of sub-dialect I were reversed, so that in II QL preceded Tag-Q. The following derivations would result:

(3)   NEG-Q Reading

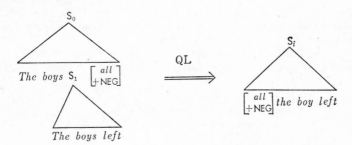

(4)   NEG-V Reading

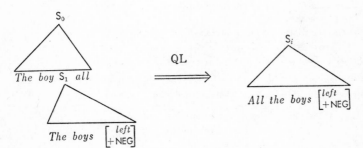

After QL, S_1 is the topmost sentence, and in both the NEG-Q and NEG-V readings S_1 is negative and will therefore take a positive tag.[3] Thus when Tag-Q applies both readings will get the positive *did they?* tag.

(5) a. Not all the boys left, did they?
     b. All the boys didn't leave, did they?

The NEG-Q reading will appear as either (5a) or (5b) in surface structure, depending on whether Quantifier NEG-Moving[4] has applied to move the NEG from the quantifier to the main verb. The NEG-V reading will appear only as (5b).

Sub-dialect AMB_{II}, in which (2)=(5b) is ambiguous between NEG-Q and NEG-V readings, is thus accounted for by the rule ordering QL before Tag-Q. We saw before that sub-dialect AMB_I required the opposite order, so that the difference between these sub-dialects can be described as a difference in rule ordering:

---

[3] This discussion evades the difficult question of exactly how the Tag-Q rule is to work. The derivation given applies to those speakers of sub-dialect AMB_{II} for whom (5a) is grammatical; if any speakers of sub-dialect AMB_{II} find (5a) ungrammatical, we should conclude that for them Tag-Q required not merely an overt NEG in the topmost S outside the tag, but also that NEG be attached to the main verb. With QNM (see footnote 4) ordered before Tag-Q, such speakers would still be able to get the required two readings of (2) and (5b).

The question of when a sentence is "negative" for the Tag-Q rule remains unsolved. Any solution will have to take into account those dialects in which grammaticality patterns ike those below appear.

(F1) a. The boys didn't not leave, did they?
      b. *The boys didn't not leave, didn't they?
      c. The boys díd not leave, didn't they?
(F2) a. Not many of the boys left, did they?
      b. *Few of the boys left, did they?
      c. *Few of the boys left, didn't they?

This data suggests that some surface-structure constraint may be involved in addition to the Tag-Q rule itself.

[4] If we assume that the NEG is attached to the quantifier before QL applies, an optional rule of Quantifier-NEG-Moving (QNM) will be required to move the NEG from the quantifier to the main verb in the NEG-Q and AMB dialects:

(F3) Not all the boys left. $\xRightarrow{\text{QNM}}$ All the boys didn't leave.

The rule is obligatory in case the quantifier phrase is in object position:

(F3′) *The boys hit not all the balls. $\xRightarrow{\text{QNM}}$
                          The boys didn't hit all the balls.

For further discussion, see Carden (1968a).

AMB$_I$	AMB$_{II}$
Tag-Q	QL
QL	Tag-Q

At this point a problem appears: Consider the tree (4) representing the NEG-V reading. In the AMB$_I$ dialect, Tag-Q should be able to apply to the positive S$_0$, producing a negative tag and the output (6):

(6) All the boys didn't leave, didn't they?

Most of our informants, however, find examples like (6) ungrammatical, "double negative." Only two of the fifteen AMB$_I$ speakers find (6) grammatical, but these do find it unambiguously NEG-V, just as (2) was unambiguously NEG-Q. There is some reason to believe that (6) is blocked for most speakers by a surface-structure constraint;[5] if such a constraint can be independently motivated, our apparent problem will disappear and the two informants who do get (6) will become additional confirmation for the rule-ordering analysis.

3. The Interaction of Tag-Question with *Not*-Transportation

(7) You don't think Mary caught the train until 6 PM, do you?

Our twenty-five informants disagree on (7), as they did on (2), but the groupings defined by the two examples differ. Looking at the data chart in Figure 4.1, we see that fifteen informants find (7) grammatical (we'll call this the AMB$_{III}$ dialect) and ten find (7) ungrammatical (AMB$_{IV}$ dialect).

Consider the structure underlying (7):

(8) You think Mary caught the train

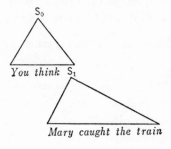

Since "caught the train" is a point-action predicate, we know by the *until* constraint that "until 6 PM" can appear in S_1 only in case S_1 is negative in underlying structure.[6] Since the NEG appears in S_0 in surface structure, we know that it was moved there by the rule of *Not*-Transportation (NT). On the other hand, since we have a positive tag in (7), S_0 must have been negative when Tag-Q applied.

It is now clear that the grammaticality of (7) depends on the relative order of Tag-Q and NT. Suppose that NT precedes Tag-Q. Then NT will move the NEG into S_0, so that S_0 is negative when Tag-Q applies. Tag-Q will therefore attach a positive tag, and the resulting surface structure is (7). Dialect AMB_{III}, in which (7) is grammatical, therefore corresponds to the rule ordering NT before Tag-Q.

Suppose instead Tag-Q precedes NT. By the *until* constraint we know that S_1 must have been negative in underlying structure, so that S_0 was positive. Since the Tag-Q rule precedes NT, S_0 will still be positive when Tag-Q applies, and a positive *do you?* tag will be blocked, making (7) ungrammatical. Dialect AMB_{IV}, in which (7) is ungrammatical, therefore corresponds to the rule ordering Tag-Q before NT.

AMB_{III}	AMB_{IV}
NT	Tag-Q
Tag-Q	NT

A problem like the one that appeared with (6) now appears with examples like (9):

(9) You don't think Mary caught the train until 6 PM, don't you?

Our analysis predicts that (9) will be good in the AMB_{IV} dialect, since Tag-Q will apply to the positive S_0 in tree (8), and so produce a negative tag "don't you?" before NT applies. (9) should therefore be as good as (10):

(10) You think Mary didn't catch the train until 6 PM, don't you?

Only three of the ten speakers of AMB_{IV}, however, find (9) grammatical. As with (6), it appears that the explanation for the seven who find (9) ungrammatical is a surface-structure constraint on double negation. If this constraint can be independently motivated, the existence of dialects in which (6) and (9) do appear with the predicted meanings will then be confirmation of the rule-order-

---

[6] See the discussion in Chapters 1 and 3, and footnote 7 to Chapter 1.

ing analysis given here.

4. Interaction among Dialects

The dialects discussed in sections 2 and 3 were defined by informant reactions to single test sentences (2) and (7). In fact, of course, any given informant will have reactions to both (2) and (7), and will therefore belong to two of the previously discussed dialects.

There are four possible combinations:

Sub-Dialect	Component Dialects	Data Set	
		(2)	(7)
W	AMB_I & AMB_{III}	NEG-Q	OK
X	AMB_I & AMB_{IV}	NEG-Q	*
Y	AMB_{II} & AMB_{III}	AMB	OK
Z	AMB_{II} & AMB_{IV}	AMB	*

For sub-dialects W and Z, the data we have already presented fully determines the relative order of NT, Tag-Q, and QL. In sub-dialect W, NT must precede Tag-Q because (7) is grammatical, and Tag-Q must precede QL because (2) has only the NEG-Q reading. The required order is therefore NT, Tag-Q, QL.

In sub-dialect Z, QL must precede Tag-Q because (2) is ambiguous and Tag-Q must precede NT because (7) is starred. The required order is therefore QL, Tag-Q, NT. Notice that in both W and Z we have determined the relative order of QL and NT indirectly, thus making a prediction about informant reactions to sentences in which QL and NT interact.

The relative rule order in sub-dialects X and Y is not fully determined by the data from (2) and (7). In X, Tag-Q must precede both NT and QL, while in Y Tag-Q must follow both NT and QL; but the relative order of NT and QL remains undetermined.

To fully specify sub-dialects X and Y, we need to get informant reactions to a sentence in which NT and QL interact directly. This will also make it possible to test the rule order we determined indirectly for sub-dialects W and Z.

(11)   John doesn't think all the boys will catch the train.

NEG-Q Reading: John thinks that not all the boys will catch the train.
NEG-V Reading: John thinks that all the boys will miss (not catch) the train.

The interpretation of (11) depends crucially on the relative order of NT and QL. If NT precedes QL, the argument in Chapter 1 holds: NT can move a NEG only from the topmost embedded S, that is, from S_1 of the trees below. The NEG construed with the quantifier in (12) can therefore be moved by NT, but the NEG construed with "catch" in (13) cannot. If NT precedes QL, therefore, (11) will have only the NEG-Q reading.

If QL precedes NT, the following derivations result:

(12)   NEG-Q Reading

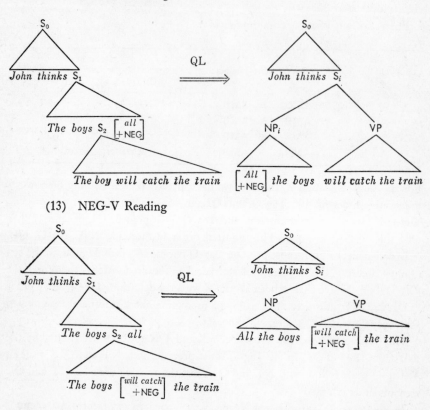

(13)   NEG-V Reading

After QL, S_1 is the topmost embedded S, and in both the NEG-Q and NEG-V readings S_1 has a negative availabe for NT.[7] If QL precedes NT, therefore, (11) will be ambiguous between the NEG-Q and NEG-V readings.

[7] Notice that this analysis requires that, after QL, a NEG on "all" and a NEG on "catch the train" must be equally available for NT. We saw in dialect AMB_{II} that Tag-Q must work the same way, since after QL a NEG on "all" and a NEG on "left" both trigger a positive tag. This suggests that there is some common definition of "negative S" at work, and thus indirectly supports our analysis.

This analysis forces some predictions about how informant responses to (2) and (7) will agree with responses to (11). No prediction is made about sub-dialects X and Y, since the relative rule order is determined for them only by the response to (11). For sub-dialect W, where the indirect ordering argument showed that NT precedes QL, all informants must find (11) unambiguously NEG-Q. For sub-dialect Z, where the indirect argument showed that QL preceded NT, all informants must find (11) ambiguous between NEG-Q and NEG-V readings. Referring to Figure 4.1, we see that these predictions check with the data, confirming the ordering analysis.

W	X	Y	Z
NT	TQ	NT, QL	QL
TQ			TQ
QL	NT, QL	TQ	NT

5.   Attested, Possible and Impossible Dialects

In section 4 we saw that all four of the possible combinations of the $AMB_{I \& II}$ and $AMB_{III \& IV}$ dialects were actually attested. Since our explanation involved the relative ordering of three rules, however, it follows that $3! = 6$ different orderings and so, in theory, six different sub-dialects are possible. This corresponds to the observation that the relative order of QL and NT was undetermined in the X and Y sub-dialects. Referring to Figure 4.1 again, we see that both orders are attested in Y, but only the NT, QL order is attested in X. That is, five of the six theoretically possible sub-dialects are attested in the sample:

Possible Sub-Dialects:

S-D	Rule Order Required	Data Set			Number of Informants
		(2)	(7)	(11)	
W	NT, Tag-Q, QL	NEG-Q	OK	NEG-Q	7
X_1	Tag-Q, NT, QL	NEG-Q	*	NEG-Q	8
Y_1	NT, QL, Tag-Q	AMB	OK	NEG-Q	4
Z	QL, Tag-Q, NT	AMB	*	AMB	2
Y_2	QL, NT, Tag-Q	AMB	OK	AMB	3
X_2	Tag-Q, QL, NT	NEG-Q	*	AMB	none

Because of the apparent rarity of informants who find (11) ambiguous between NEG-Q and NEG-V readings, it is perhaps not a serious fault that our analysis predicts the existence of the as-yet-unattested sub-dialect X_2.[8]

A more serious complaint might be that this method of explanation by rule ordering is too powerful, that it appears that any arbitrary data could be explained, so that there is no way to falsify the proposed analysis. Such a complaint would be based on a miscalculation. In fact there are $2^3 = 8$ possible combinations of data from the particular examples we have been concerned with, and only $3! = 6$ possible rule orders within our analysis. Thus there are two possible sets of informant reactions to (2), (7), and (11) that would disprove our analysis:

Allegedly Impossible Sub-Dialects:

S-D	Rule Order Required	Data Set			Attested?
		(2)	(7)	(11)	
S	NT, QL, Tag-Q, NT	AMB	*	NEG-Q	no
T	QL, NT, Tag-Q, QL	NEG-Q	OK	AMB	no

S is impossible, even with a cycle, because NT would be able to apply to the output of QL, thus making sentences of the type (11) ambiguous and contradicting the assumption that (11) was unambiguous. T is likewise impossible, because Tag-Q would be able to apply to the output of QL, making (2) AMB and contradicting the assumption that (2) was unambiguously NEG-Q.

Our analysis thus makes it possible to divide the 8 mathematically possible data sets into attested sub-dialects (W, X, Y_1, Y_2, Z), possible but unattested sub-dialects (X_2), and impossible sub-dialects (S, T).

6. Conclusion

In the preceding sections we have seen how data from only three sample sentences makes it possible to divide the AMB dialect into five attested subdialects, and how the differences among these sub-dialects can be explained by the assumption that the speakers' grammars differ in the ordering of three transformations.

At this stage it is reasonable to ask what cause can be assigned to this apparently near-random ordering of transformations. The sub-dialects do not appear to correlate with any geographical or sociological characteristics of their speakers;

---

[8] While it may be a coincidence, it is suspicious that dialect X, where (2) is unambiguously NEG-Q, does not have a sub-dialect X_2 in which (11) has both NEG-Q and NEG-V readings. This asymmetry between the X and Y dialects is unexplained by my analysis. Bailey (1970a) offers a possible explanation based on marked and unmarked rule order and the hypothesis that a partial unmarking of rule order is forbidden.

from the limited data available it seems that the variation is in fact random.

If our description is right, and these dialects do in fact differ only in rule order, we can offer a speculative explanation for the randomness: Linguists have often found it difficult to construct solid arguments to show that one rule order is preferred to another. It is reasonable to suppose that the language learner has similar difficulties. In examples like those we have considered, the language learner might well have a reasonable amount of evidence about the existence and form of the QL, Tag-Q, and NT rules, but little if any evidence for their relative order, since the crucial sentences that determine the order are likely to be of low frequency. If we assume that the language learner has to order his rules, and assigns an arbitrary order whenever he has no evidence as to which order is preferred, we then approach an explanation for the apparently arbitrary distribution of these dialects.

Chapter 5:

Dialect Variation and Linguistic Change[1]

1. Introduction

In Chapter 3 we merely described the dialect pattern of sentences like "All the boys didn't leave" without attempting to explain them. The three dialects we described differed in the relative scope they assigned to "all" and "not," so that an explanation of the differences, if one can be found, will have to be based on a theory of the way the scope of logical predicates like quantifiers and negatives is determined.

In this chapter we consider two recent hypotheses about scope determination, and show how a consideration of dialect evidence casts doubt on both of them. The evidence also shows that dialects potentially differ in derivational constraints or in interpretive semantic rules as well as in ordinary syntactic rules. While the evidence does not lead to a clear and satisfactory solution of the scope problem, arguments based on certain plausible assumptions about the nature of linguistic change suggest that the method of derivational constraints is more promising than the method of interpretive semantic rules.

The form of argument used suggests a promising approach to the synchronic relevance of diachronic evidence.

2. The Scope Problem

    (1)   a.   All the marksmen didn't hit the target.

[1] This chapter is a slightly revised version of "A Problem with Primacy," originally published in *Linguistic Inquiry* 1:526–33 (1970).

    b.   The target wasn't hit by all the marksmen.

Reading A: $\forall$ (m ε the marksmen) [∼(Hit (m, the target))]

Reading B: ∼[$\forall$ (m ε the marksmen) (Hit (m, the target))]

At first glance sentences like (1a) and (1b) seem to be derived from the same deep or underlying structure using the Passive transformation. For many speakers, however, (1a) and (1b) have no reading in common. In this NEG-V dialect, (1a) means only 1A and (1b) means only 1B. Readings 1A and 1B differ in the relative scope of "all" and "not": in 1A "all" includes "not" in its scope; in 1B "not" includes "all" in its scope. The problem of explaining the difference in meaning between sentences like (1a) and (1b), therefore, is the problem of explaining how the scope of logical predicates like "all" and "not" is determined.

3. The Primacy-Relation Solution

Jackendoff (1969b) and Lakoff (1969) have recently attacked this problem. Despite their theoretical differences, their proposed solutions share some essential features; in this chapter I shall be concerned with their claim that the scope of logical predicates is marked by "shallow-structure primacy relations,"[2] and with difficulties that arise when their solution is extended to dialects other than the ones they describe.[3]

Jackendoff noticed that, in his NEG-V dialect, the shallow-structure linear order of logical predicates is the same as the "understood order." In his system, "understood order" in semantic structure determines scope; it apparently corresponds, at least for purposes of scope determination, to the quantification theory representations given in 1A and 1B. Thus in (1) we see that the linear order of "all" and "not" is the same in (1a) and its reading 1A, and likewise for (1b) and

---

[2] "Primacy relation" appears first in Langacker (1969); Lakoff (1969) applies this term to the three relations (linear order, asymmetrical command, and extra-heavy stress) that he finds mark scope differences. Though Jackendoff (1969b) does not use the term, his linear-order relation fits Langacker's original definition.

I use Lakoff's term "shallow structure" to mean the level on which the primacy relations are defined. Jackendoff says "The scope rule will take as its input some fairly late level of derived structure, perhaps even surface structure" (1969b p 241), so the use of Lakoff's term seems fair in this case. The differences between shallow structure and surface structure are not relevant to my arguments, and in fact all examples have been chosen so that their shallow and surface structures are identical.

[3] Jackendoff limits himself to the NEG-V dialect. Lakoff mentions the AMB dialect and a sub-dialect in which extra-heavy stress is relevant, but concentrates on the NEG-V dialect of Jackendoff. It is to Lakoff's credit that he says explicitly how his rules would differ for the different dialects.

1B.

Jackendoff proposes to express this insight by an "interpretive rule," under which difference of scope in semantic structure is determined by shallow-structure linear order. This rule can be paraphrased as:

Rule I: If logical predicate P_1 precedes logical predicate P_2 in shallow structure, then P_1 includes P_2 in its scope.

Lakoff shows that Jackendoff's insight can be expressed equally well by a "derivational constraint," under which the shallow-structure linear order is determined by the difference of scope in semantic structure. He also points out two exceptions to Jackendoff's Rule I, and proposes to account for them by additional primacy relations.

(2)   The marksmen who didn't hit the target were many.
     Reading A: MANY (m ε the marksmen) [~(Hit (m, the target))]
     Reading B: ~[MANY (m ε the marksmen) (Hit (m, the target))]

In (2), for example, "not" precedes "many," so Rule I predicts that the meaning will be 2B. In fact, however, (2) only means 2A. Lakoff notes that "many" is in a higher S than "not," and proposes that this "asymmetrical command"[4] marks the difference in scope. As a second exception, Lakoff describes a sub-dialect in which scope is marked by "extra-heavy stress."

To explain these exceptions, Lakoff proposes a hierarchy of primacy relations, with asymmetrical command over-riding extra-heavy stress, and extra-heavy stress over-riding linear order. This system, which he expresses in derivational constraints, can be paraphrased as:

Rule II: If logical predicate P_1 includes logical predicate P_2 in its scope, then
     a. P_1 has asymmetrical command over P_2 in shallow structure; or
     b.   If (a) does not apply, P_1 has extra-heavy stress; or
     c.   If neither (a) nor (b) applies, P_1 precedes P_2 in the shallow-structure string.

It is clear that Lakoff's refinements can be adapted to Jackendoff's system of interpretive rules, so that the facts considered to date offer no evidence bearing

---

[4] The notion of "command" is due to Langacker (1969). Node A "commands" node B if and only if the first S-node dominating A also dominates B. Node X "asymmetrically commands" node Y if and only if X commands Y and Y does not command X. Note that "asymmetrical command" is defined in terms of dominance in a P-marker, and is therefore a primacy relation in Langacker's sense.

on a choice between interpretive rules and derivational constraints. For example, Rule IIc is equivalent to Jackendoff's Rule I, so that the two analyses agree for the case in which both logical predicates are in the same shallow S (i.e., neither has asymmetrical command) and neither has extra-heavy stress.

4. Counter-Examples[5]

In this chapter we are concerned with the claim that scope is marked by primacy relations at the shallow-structure level. This claim can be refuted by showing examples where scope is independent of any shallow-structure primacy relation. We must therefore ask what a primacy relation is. As Langacker originally used the term, primacy relations were defined over "structural relations in a P-marker (linear ordering and dominance relations)."[6] "Precedes" and "asymmetrically commands" fit this definition. "Extra-heavy stress" does not,[7] but intuitively seems to have something in common with order and dominance as a means of emphasis. Thus, though neither Lakoff or Jackendoff has published a formal definition of "primacy relation," we have a certain feel for the sort of thing that can be a primacy relation. In particular, primacy relations are in some sense structural; for example, a rule of scope determination of the form "lexical item X includes lexical item Y in its scope" would not be said to be based on a primacy relation.

4.1 Counter-Example I

So far our discussion of scope determination has been limited to the NEG-V dialect. Let us consider now the NEG-Q dialect, in which (1a) means unambiguously 1B. This result is the opposite of that predicted by Jackendoff's Rule I or Lakoff's Rule IIc.

Since it seems plausible that interpretive rules or derivational constraints can vary from dialect to dialect, one might propose that scope was always marked by linear order, but that NEG-Q dialect had a different marking rule, say interpretive rule I':

Rule I':   If logical predicate P_1 precedes logical predicate P_2 in the

---

[5] In all the counter-examples, the stress is normal and both logical predicates appear in the same shallow-structure S. Thus Lakoff's and Jackendoff's analyses have the same effect for all the counter-examples.

[6] Langacker (1969 p 185).

[7] There is, however, some evidence suggesting that contrastive stress marks underlying dominance: "*John* ran."="It was John who ran." Here the contrastively stressed "*John*" in the first sentence corresponds to the higher-S "John" in the second.

shallow-structure string, then P_2 includes P_1 in its scope.

A similar revision of Lakoff's analysis would reverse Rule IIc.

This solution works for (1a), but gives the wrong result for sentences like (1b) or (3):

> (3)   The marksman didn't hit all the targets.
> Reading A: V (t ε the targets) [∼(Hit (the marksman, t))]
> Reading B: ∼[V (t ε the targets) (Hit (the marksman, t))]

In the NEG-Q dialect, (1b) means only 1B, not 1A as predicted by Rule I'. Likewise, (3) means 3B, not 3A.

In all three sentences, (1a), (1b), and (3), "not" includes "all" in its scope. In (1a) the linear order is "all . . . not," in (1b) and (3) it is "not . . . all." It is plain that, in this dialect and for these examples, the relative scope of "All" and "not" is independent of shallow-structure linear order. How, then, is scope marked? Asymmetrical command and extra-heavy stress do not apply, and the identical behavior of (1b) and (3) shows that the Passive is not involved.

When Lakoff discovered exceptions to Jackendoff's Rule I, there were obvious structural differences between the exceptions and the non-exceptions; the structural differences could be described as new primacy relations that over-rode linear order. Here there is no obvious new primacy relation to be discovered; no obvious way in which (1b) and (3) differ from (1a) that could over-ride the hypothesized influence of the linear order. The best that can be done at this stage is an *ad hoc* description:

> Rule III: (NEG-Q dialect) If "all" and "not" appear in the same
>   shallow-structure S, then "not" includes "all" in its scope.

4.2 Counter-Example II

> (4)   Every marksman didn't hit the target.
> (5)   Each marksman didn't hit the target.

In the NEG-Q dialect, "every" acts like "all," so that (4) and (1a) both mean unambiguously 1B. "Each" is different: (5) means unambiguously 1A even in the NEG-Q dialect.[8]

---

[8] Baker (1970a) points out that "some" "and perhaps . . . a small number of other quantifiers" act in the way I have described for "each," and are thus exceptions to Jackendoff's Rule I. Baker's proposed solution is that "the condition on understood order and surface structure order is a condition that simply marks as less acceptable any sentence in which the two orders do not agree."

Again the relative scope is independent of the shallow-structure linear order. In both (4) and (5) the linear order is "Quantifier . . . not," but in (4) "not" includes the quantifier in its scope, and in (5) the quantifier includes "not" in its scope. Since (4) and (5) differ in shallow structure only in the lexical terms "each" and "every," the only solution seems to be an *ad hoc* rule like III that refers to the individual lexical items.[9]

5. Conclusion: Rejection of the Primacy-Relation Solution

In the NEG-Q dialect the relative scopes of "each," "every," and "all" and "not" are determined independently of shallow-structure linear order and the other shallow-structure primacy relations thought to be relevant to scope determination. In counter-example I, the relative scope was constant while the linear order varied; in counterexample II the order was constant while the relative scope varied. It appears that both these examples will have to be handled by rules like Rule III, so that relative scope appears to be a property of individual lexical items.[10] Though rules like III could be stated equally well as interpretive semantic rules or as derivational constraints, they seem to be fundamentally different from rules based on structural primacy relations.[11] This suggests that

[9] It is significant that this argument can be reconstructed for the AMB dialect, where (1a) is ambiguous and means either 1A or 1B. In this dialect "every" acts like "all," so that (4) is ambiguous; but (5) means unambiguously 1A. There are thus difficulties with the primacy-relation analysis in two of the three main quantifier dialects.

The relation of "many" to this pattern is a puzzle. In some sub-dialects "many" acts like "each," in others it acts like "all" and "every." There are also some dialects in which "every" acts like "each."

There is a temptation to relate the observation that "each" is unambiguously NEG-V to the observed non-occurrence of "*not each," but comparison with the dialects in which "each" and "many" or "each" and "every" act alike suggests that this is mistaken.

[10] In a system where quantifiers and negatives are predicates of higher S's, such a rule must state that specific lexical items (e.g. "all" and "every") cannot appear as the predicate of a sentence immediately above one that has a different specific lexical item (e.g. "not") as its predicate. It is interesting that similar verb-verb constraints may be needed in the Ross (1967) analysis of the English auxiliary.

[11] Lakoff points out (personal communication) that Rule III could be paraphrased by a derivational constraint using the primacy relation "command," and that, since "asymmetrical command" is already defined in terms of command, no additional primacy relation would be needed. In fact, Lakoff could argue, the use of "in the same shallow-structure S" in Rule III is an implicit use of command, so that Rule III itself depends on a primacy relation.

The problem with Lakoff's proposed derivational constraint is that it applies to so few lexical items that the restriction to certain lexical items seems to be more central to its operation than the primacy relation.

the Jackendoff-Lakoff system of marking scope by shallow-structure primacy relations should be revised. Our objective should be a unified analysis that explains scope determination in the NEG-V and the NEG-Q dialects using similar mechanisms.

6. Towards a Solution

Given our present data, there seems little to choose between the derivational-constraint and interpretive-rule methods; and now that the primacy-relation solution has been abandoned, neither looks very attractive. Still, it is possible to find some evidence as to the direction in which an eventual solution is likely to develop.

To simplify the presentation, let us limit the discussion to cases where "all" and "not" appear in the same shallow S with normal intonation. Consider how each method will handle the three dialects:

Interpretive Semantic Rules
  NEG-V Dialect: Rule I
  NEG-Q Dialect: Rule III
  AMB Dialect: Rule I and rule III, plus some unspecified convention to ensure
      that exactly one of them applies to any given S.

Derivational Constraints
  NEG-V Dialect: Rule I
  NEG-Q Dialect: Rule III
  AMB Dialect: No constraint

It appears, then, that the AMB dialect will be the simplest of the three dialects in an analysis with derivational constraints, and the most complicated in an analysis with interpretive semantic rules.

If we assume that linguistic change normally represents a simplification of the grammar, at least at the point where the initial change takes place, two additional facts can be seen to give indirect support to the method of derivational constraints:[12]

---

[12] This argument is, of course, based on oversimplified data since we have considered only the inter-relation of "all" and "not." In fact it appears that rule I, and perhaps rule III as well, will have a wider range of application, so that it will not necessarily be the case that (e.g.) preventing rule I from applying to "all" and "not" will give a simpler grammar. Until both derivational-constraint and interpretive analyses of scope determination have been worked out in some detail, it will be possible for a partisan of either side to devise a plausible-looking analysis in which the theory he favors gives AMB the simplest grammar of the three dialects.

1. Speakers of NEG-Q have been known to change to AMB over a period
of months, no changes from AMB to NEG-Q or NEG-V have been observed.

2. AMB is the most common dialect.

We can conclude that, while the scope problem remains unsolved,[13] our present
data suggests that derivational constraints are more promising than interpretive
semantic rules.

The important point to notice is the form of argument used, rather than the
particular conclusion reached. We have taken a theory of linguistic change motivated by historical data, applied it to synchronic dialect variations, and reached
a conclusion about the synchronic analysis of the individual dialects. The synchronic analysis chosen then motivates a choice between competing semantic
theories. This sort of argument, if it proves to be widely applicable, offers an
approach to the old problem of the synchronic relevance of historical data, and
the possibility of a genuinely unified linguistic theory.

---

[13] A possible approach would be to use the same mechanism to explain the determination
of scope and the determination of focus or emphasis; that is, the plain difference in meaning between (1a) and (1b) in the NEG-V dialect and the more subtle difference between
"John kissed Mary." and "Mary was kissed by John."

It is interesting that stress, order, and dominance, which are clearly related to scope
determination, are also related to emphasis. Cf footnote 7.

Appendix A:

A Rule-Ordering Paradox[1]

1. Introduction

Standard analyses in generative grammar have regarded the anaphora rules of Pronominalization, Equi-NP Deletion, and Reflexive as operating on identical, co-referential noun phrases. Recently, however, various paradoxes have been found that show that this standard NP-identity analysis is inadequate and must be replaced by some (as-yet-undiscovered) more powerful mechanism. Thus Bach (1970) has shown that, given the usual analysis of Pronominalization, certain sentences will require infinite underlying structures; and a similar but independent *reductio ad infinitum* has recently been discovered for pronominalization to *some* and *these*.[2] Similarly, Postal (1970) has shown that the usual NP-identity analysis of Equi-NP Deletion leads to an ordering paradox in which Equi-NP Deletion must be both cyclic and last- or non-cyclic. In this appendix I show that the usual NP-identity analysis of Reflexive leads to a similar ordering paradox, in which Quantifier Lowering must be both cyclic and last- or non-cyclic.

There are various ways to escape from these paradoxes, for example Postal's proposal that Equi-NP Deletion be divided into a cyclic rule of Doom-Marking and a last- or non-cyclic rule of Doom-Erasure, but none of the individual escape routes is very appealing. When one considers that one must escape simultaneously from all the paradoxes in order to maintain an NP-identity analysis of anaphora, it becomes clear that the only acceptable solution is a new way of han-

[1] David Perlmutter and Susumu Kuno independently noticed the interaction of Raising and QL (section 2.2) which led to the discovery of this paradox.
[2] Carden and Miller (1970).

dling anaphora.[3]

2. QL is cyclic

In the body of the thesis I have used the non-cyclic rule-ordering convention. This assumption makes it possible to state certain generalizations that could not be handled with the cyclic convention, as we shall see shortly; but it is not compatible with the usual NP-Identity rule of Reflexive.

2.1 Reflexive

A first approximation to the internal structure of the higher S before QL was given in Chapter 1; if we apply that first approximation to a sentence like (1), we get the following underlying structure:

(1) All the men$_i$ hate all the men$_i$.

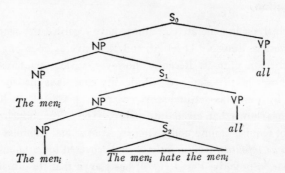

Suppose now that Reflexive applies before QL. Then Reflexive will operate in S_2, and the output will be something like "All the men hate themselves all," with no way to get (1). If Reflexive applies after QL (say in the S_0 cycle) the situation is even worse, since the output will be "All the men hate themselves," which means something quite different.

What appears to be needed is a more complicated structure with some of the power of the logician's variables. This second-approximation underlying structure might look like this, where NP_q represents the set quantified over.[4]

(2) All the boys left.

---

[3] Improved analyses of anaphora have been proposed by Jackendoff (1969a) and in numerous papers by McCawley (e.g. (1970)); Grinder and Postal (1971) offer a valuable evaluation of two possible theories.

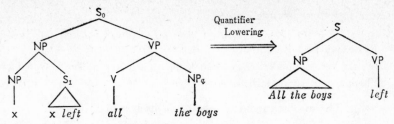

When we apply this to (1), with the order Reflexive before QL, we find that the derivation presents no problems:

(1)   All the men$_i$ hate all the men$_i$.

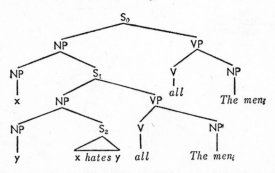

Reflexive is blocked at all stages, and we get the desired output. An additional advantage is that this underlying structure seems to represent accurately informants' intuitions about the meaning of (1): that the primary meaning is that each man hates each other man (x hates y), but that the case where he hates himself is included incidentally or accidentally (the case where x=y).

If we are to generate sentences like (1) using an NP-Identity rule of Reflexive, we must (a) order Reflexive before QL and (b) develop a variable underlying

---

[4] While the variable is represented here as a plain "x," it is clear that it will have to carry the selectional features of NP$_q$, so that at the least "x" represents a feature bundle. Examples like (F1) suggests that "x" may itself be a lexical noun or even a full NP:

(F1)   a.   The boys—every one of them—fled.   (one=boy)
          b.   The army—every man of it—fled.

See Carden (1968a) for further discussion of such sentences. The crucial point for the second-approximation structure is that "x" bears an index unequal to that of "y" or NP$_q$.

Sentences like (F2) suggest that the variable underlying structure of (2) cannot be used for those quantifiers like "few" and "many" that appear in Overt-Predicate position:

(F2)   John expects the boys who win to be few.

Here it must be possible to raise "the boys" before QL applies, an analysis that plainly won't work with the variable deep structure. This conclusion casts doubt on the whole variable approach developed here, as does the conclusion at the end of section 2.2.

structure something like the one in (2).

2.2 Reflexive and Raising.

Given the variable underlying structure of (2), a sentence like (3) would have the following underlying structure:

(3) The royalist candidates expect themselves to all win.

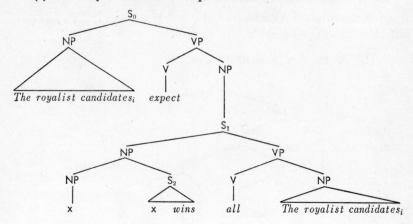

To generate (3) from this underlying structure, rules must apply in the following order: QL in S_1, QM* in S_1, Raising in S_0, and Reflexive in S_0. In the previous section, however, we saw that Reflexive must apply before QL. These two rule orders can be reconciled only if both Reflexive and QL are cyclic, with Reflexive preceding QL in the cycle. The rules will then apply as follows (vacuous application indicated by parentheses):

S_2 cycle: (Raising) (Reflexive) (QL) (QM)
S_1 cycle: (Raising) (Reflexive) QL QM
S_0 cycle: Raising Reflexive (QL) (QM)

We can add to the conclusions of section 2.1 the further conclusion that both Reflexive and QL are cyclic.

Suppose now we try to generate a more complicated sentence like (4), combining some of the properties of (1) and (3). Such sentences will require an additional refinement in the structure proposed in (2).

---

* The Quantifier-Moving rules (QM) move a pre-determiner quantifier around its NP and (in some cases) into the VP :

(F3) All the boys have left. $\overset{QM}{=\!=\!=\!\Rightarrow}$ The boys have all left See Appendix B, sections 2.1 and 5.1 and Carden (1968a).

(4) All the royalist candidates expect themselves to all win.

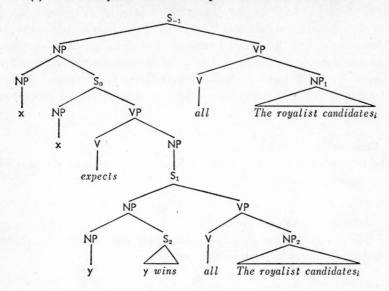

The derivation of this sentence will take the same path as that of (3) until we get to Reflexive in S_0:

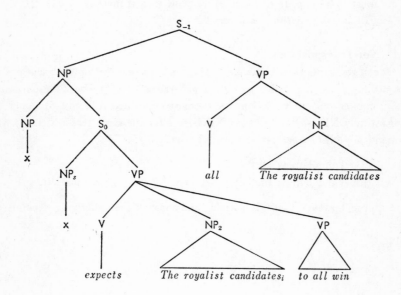

Here the raised NP_2 "the royalist candidates" cannot reflexivize, since it is not equal to the subject NP_s "x". It appears that we can generate sentences like (4) within our existing framework only if we permit NP_2 in underlying structure to be a variable equal to "x". While I know of no evidence against this proposal, it does cast some doubt on the plausibility of the analysis that we have been forced into by the NP-Identity rule of Reflexive. Notice that the first-approximation underlying structure that failed on (1) would work perfectly well for (3) and (4).

2.3 Conclusion

The hypothesis that there is a rule of Reflexive operating on identical NPs leads to three conclusions:

1. There is a cycle.
2. Reflexive and QL are cyclic.
3. The pre-QL structure of the quantifiers must make extensive use of some mechanism equivalent to the logician's variables.

3. QL is Last-Cyclic

In the previous section we saw that the interaction of QL and NP-Identity Reflexive required that QL and Reflexive both be cyclic, and so of course that there must be a cycle. In this section we show that, if there is a cycle, QL must be last cyclic, thus deriving a contradiction.

3.1 *Not*-Transportation

One of the strongest arguments for QL has been that the higher-S analysis of quantifiers made it possible to state a generalization that *Not*-Transportation (NT) applied only to a NEG in the topmost embedded S. Thus (5) would be semantically NEG-*all* rather than NEG-*leave* for the same reason that (6) was semantically NEG-*leave* rather than NEG-*enjoying*:

(5) I don't think all the boys left.
(6) I don't think the boys who were enjoying themselves left.

Suppose, however, that QL is cyclic, and consider the underlying structure of (5):

(5')

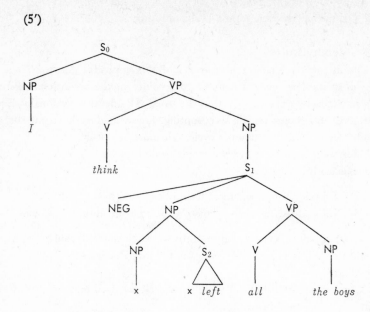

After the S_1 cycle, QL will have applied, and if Quantifier-NEG-Moving[5] also has applied the structure will be something like this:

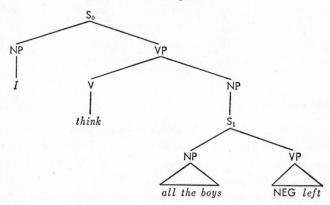

There will then be no non-*ad-hoc* way for NT to distinguish a NEG that originally modified "all" from one that originally modified "leave,"[6] and the generalization about quantifiers and NT will be lost.

If QL is last cyclic, or if there is no cycle, then all that is required is that NT

---

[5] See footnote 4 to Chapter 4 for discussion of Quantifier-NEG-Moving.

[6] It is important to notice that in sub-dialect Z (Chapter 4), where QL precedes NT, NT would apply to a NEG that semantically modified "leave" in (5).

precede QL in the last cycle or non-cyclic ordering.

3.2 NP-Identity Rules

We saw in chapter 1 and in section 2.1 of this appendix that the higher-S analysis of quantifiers made it possible to account for the anomalous behavior of NPs modified by quantifiers within the usual NP-Identity versions of Equi-NP Deletion and Reflexive. This accounting, however, depended crucially on the rule-ordering used: if there is a cycle, QL must be last-cyclic.

Consider what happens when we embed sentences like (1) in a matrix S so as to get an additional cycle:

(7) Jill said that all the men$_i$ hate all the men$_i$.
(8) Jill said that all the optimists$_i$ expect all the optimists$_i$ to win.

The derivation will proceed as before until we reach the "Jill said S" cycle. At that point we shall have no non-*ad-hoc* way to block Reflexive in (7) or Equi-NP Deletion in (8).

Again, if QL is last cyclic or if there is no cycle we need only order Reflexive and Equi-NP Deletion before QL.

3.3 Conclusion

We appear to be caught in an ordering paradox, in which QL must be both cyclic (section 2.2) and last-cyclic or non-cyclic (sections 3.1 and 3.2).

It is especially significant that the very rule of Reflexive that required QL to be cyclic (section 2.2) also requires QL to be last cyclic (section 3.2).

4. Possible escapes

There are several possible ways to escape from the paradox developed in the preceding sections. In this section I consider these possibilities, and show that each leads to a loss of significant generalizations. After balancing the disadvantages, the best solution appears to be to reject the NP-identity analysis of Reflexive, and so avoid the necessity of a cyclic QL. This is in line with the independent evidence that NP-identity analyses of anaphora are unsatisfactory.

4.1 Making QL cyclic: The NT Argument

One might propose that the meaning of sentences like (5) be controlled by a derivational constraint like those described in Lakoff (1969), so that the order of embedding at the time NT applied was irrelevant, and all that mattered was the order of embedding in underlying structure.

There are three problems with this proposal. 1. You lose the generalization that (5) and (6) are controlled by the same mechanism. 2. You lose the explanation that the rarity of sub-dialect Z (Chapter 4) is correlated with the rarity of the dialect in which (5) can have a NEG-V reading, and that in fact the two dialects can only occur together. 3. As stated it won't work: Consider a sentence like (9):

> (9)   a.   John doesn't expect all the boys to leave.
>   b.   The marksman didn't hit all the targets.

Since the NEG and the "all" are in the same S, the derivational-constraint analysis predicts that the meaning of (9a) would show the same dialect variations as (9b). But this is false: there is a dialect in which (9a) is AMB and (9b) is NEG-Q only, and a possible dialect (only one informant) in which (9a) is only NEG-Q and (9b) is AMB.

It might be possible to save the derivational-constraint solution if we made the additional requirement that the constraint must hold at all levels of intermediate structure as well as at shallow-structure. Then, if NT precedes Raising, there would be a stage after NT when the "not" asymmetrically commanded the "all," thus blocking the NEG-V reading.

Even if we make this move, we are still left with the first two problems. At the present level of analysis the solution without the derivational constraint seems preferable, but it is important to notice the independently-motivated derivational constraint itself includes a notion of underlying embedding, so that one should hope eventually to be able to state some broader generalization that would bring the two solutions together.[7]

4.2   Making QL-cyclic: The NP-Identity Argument

Haj Ross (personal communication) points out that the problem in 3.2 can be evaded if we can state Equi-NP Deletion and Reflexive in such a way that they can apply only in the topmost S. That is, they would have to be stated so that the controlling NP was the subject of the topmost S the cycle was operating on. This places stringent requirements on the ordering of these rules; in particular, they would have to apply before any transformations that wiped out higher Ss, and thus before QL and all performative-lowering transformations. Since we know already that they must apply before QL, this is not a wholly

---

[7] The claim that there is some broader generalization underlying both the derivation constraint and the highest-S analysis of NT is supported by the observation that at least one speaker of Sub-Dialect Z finds (F4) ambiguous between NEG-V and NEG-Q readings:

(F4)   It is not the case that all the boys left.

improbable requirement, but we shall have to learn more about performatives before we can tell if such a solution is workable.

Any proposal to handle this problem will have to take into account the existence of at least one speaker for whom it appears that Reflexive applies freely to quantified NPs.[8] For him, (10a) is out and (10b) has a reading synonymous with (10a), whereas (11a), with a very similar pre-QL structure in our analysis, is quite all right.

(10) a. All the bureaucrats hate all the bureaucrats.

       b. All the bureaucrats hate themselves.

(11) a. Each man on the general staff respects all the men on the general staff.

4.3 A New Sort of Reflexive

It is interesting and significant that all the known arguments for the transformational cycle depend on some property of anaphora.[9] To the extent that we

[8] If this evidence is supported by additional data and confirmed by other informants, it should disprove the hypothesis that NP anaphora rules apply only to variables within the scope of a quantifier and never to full NPs.

[9] One apparent exception is the Lakoff (1967) argument involving Raising and Passive. Consider sentences like (F5):

(F5) a. Mary was expected by Jack to have been seen by Jane to have been defeated by Jill.

       b. Jack expected that Jane would have seen that Jill defeated Mary.

Here, the argument goes, (F5a) must have been derived from (F5b) by cyclical application of Raising and Passive in that order. Since Passive in S_2 must precede Raising in S_1, and Passive in S_1 must follow Raising in S_1, we conclude that there must be a cycle. It appears that this conclusion is independent of the anaphora rules.

Lakoff points out, however, that there is an alternate, non-cyclic analysis that fails only because it cannot handle certain cross-over facts. Suppose, starting from (F5b), we passivize everywhere. This gives (F6):

(F6) That that Mary would be defeated by Jill would have been seen by Jane was expected by Jack.

We can then extrapose, using the rule independently required for *seem* sentences like (F7), and get (F5a).

(F7) a. *That that Mary would be defeated by Jill would have been seen by Jane seemed.

       b. Mary seemed to have been seen by Jane to have been defeated by Jill.

This non-cyclic analysis fails only because it cannot block sentences like: (F8):

(F8) *Mary was expected by herself to have won.

In the cyclic analysis the cross-over principle will block Passive in S_0, but in the non-cyclic analysis the whole noun clause will move during Passive and cross-over will not apply. Thus we see that the Raising-Passive argument for the cycle does in fact depend indirectly on anaphora phenomena.

can regard the existing analysis of Reflexive as a firmly-established rule, the arguments for a cyclic QL in section 1 are sound, and we must abandon QL or take the escape routes in sections 4.1 and 4.2. But given the known paradoxes to which Pronominalization and Equi-NP Deletion have led to, it seems more plausible to blame our present paradox on Reflexive rather than on QL. Without being able to suggest any specific general analysis for anaphora phenomena, it seems plausible to hope that when an analysis is found that solves the paradoxes with Pronominalization and Equi-NP Deletion, that analysis will also solve this paradox with Reflexive.

Appendix B:

The Deep Structure of "Both"[1]

1. Introduction

At first glance "both" seems to be a quantifier like "all" or "each"; it appears in the same surface structures and acts similarly under certain transformations. On the other hand, there are many examples where "both" acts unlike the quantifiers, and the arguments in Lakoff and Peters (1966) suggest that "both" should be derived from an underlying sentence conjunction.

In this paper I investigate this apparent contradiction. Examples where "both" modifies predicates seem to show conclusively that "both" cannot have the same underlying structure as the quantifiers, but then the examples where "both" does act like a quantifier remain to be explained. It develops that the sentence-conjunction analysis, when combined with a quantifier derived structure, will handle the data that originally motivated the quantifier analysis. The derived structure and approximate rule-order that are used for this purpose are needed in any case to account for the behavior of predicate-modifying "both," which could not possibly come from underlying quantifiers.

The conclusion that "both" comes from an underlying conjunction is not a new one; the NED (1888) mentions that it is usual to classify "both" as a conjunction because of the parallel with constructions like the Latin *et . . . et . . .* (For us, of course, the observation that the word corresponding to "both" in

[1] This section is a slightly revised version of a paper of the same title originally published in *Papers from the Sixth Regional Meeting of the Chicago Linguistic Society* (1970).

I am grateful to Susumu Kuno and David Perlmutter, who read earlier versions of this chapter and made many helpful suggestions. My mistakes, of course, are my own, and neither of my advisors necessarily agrees with anything I say.

many languages is overtly a conjunction is suggestive rather than probative.) What is interesting is that the resulting analysis shows that the conjunction underlying "both" has some of the "higher-predicate" properties of quantifiers, and suggests the generalization that quantifiers and conjunctions form a natural class of "logical predicates."

2. "Both" as a Quantifier

2.1 Surface-Structure Parallels

"Both" appears in a number of surface-structures that are usually regarded as characteristic of quantifiers:

(1) a. All ((of) the) boys have left.
      b. The boys all (of them) have left.
      c. The boys have all (of them) left.
(2) a. Both ((of) the) boys have left.
      b. The boys both (of them) have left.
      c. The boys have both (of them) left.

The (a) structure is usually taken as basic, with the (b) and (c) structures derived from it by Quantifier-Moving rules.[2]

2.2 Deeper Parallels

"Both" acts like the quantifiers under Equi-NP Deletion and *Not*-Transportation, so that the arguments for a higher-S analysis of quantifiers in Chapter 1 also apply to "both."

Equi-NP Deletion
(3) a. All the candidates expect all the candidates to win.
      b. All the candidates expect to win.
(4) a. Both the candidates expect both the candidates to win.
      b. Both the candidates expect to win.

Where the "candidates" in the (a) sentences are co-referential, one would expect the (a) sentences to reduce to the (b) sentences. But this is impossible since the

---

[2] See Carden (1968a) for details. David Perlmutter points out (personal communication) that the existence of dialects in which (F1b) is grammatical and (F1a) is not casts doubt on this Quantifier-Moving rule analysis.

  (F1) a. *All the guests began to arrive.
        b. The guests all began to arrive.

See also example (11), p. 92.

(a) and (b) sentences are not synonymous. We conclude that they must have different underlying structures.

Not-*Transportation*

(5) a. I don't think all the boys left.
     b. I think it is not the case that all the boys left.
     c. I think all the boys stayed.
(6) a. I don't think both the boys left.
     b. I think it is not the case that both the boys left.
     c. I think both the boys stayed.

We notice that in both (5) and (6) the (a) sentences have a reading synonymous with the equivalent (b) sentences, but no reading synonymous with the (c) sentences. It appears that *Not*-Transportation can apply in such sentences only in case the "not" to be transported semantically modifies the quantifier or "both."

In these examples, as in section 2.1, we see "both" acting like a quantifier; whatever the merits of the higher-S analysis of quantifiers, there seems to be a generalization in treating "both" as a quantifier.

3. "Both" as a Non-Quantifier

3.1 Lakoff-Peters Examples

The arguments in Lakoff and Peters (1966) can be recast to give information on the underlying structure of "both." Notice first that "both" does not appear with certain predicates, though "all" and the other plural quantifiers are acceptable:

(7) a. All the men met at noon.
     b. *Both the men met at noon.
     c. *Both Tom and Bill met at noon.
     d. Tom and Bill met at noon.

Other predicates are disambiguated when "both" is added:

(8) a. John and Bronwyn married.
         Reading 1—John married Bronwyn
         Reading 2—John married X and Bronwyn married Y
     b. Both John and Bronwyn married.

(8b) has only reading 2.

Now notice that sentence conjunctions act the same way as the sentences with "both":

(7) b'. *Man$_1$ met at noon and man$_2$ met at noon.

    c'. *Tom met at noon and Bill met at noon.

(8) b'. John married and Bronwyn married.

(8b') has only reading 2.

This suggests that there is a generalization in deriving sentences with "both" from a sentence conjunction.

3.2 Miscellaneous Examples

"Both" also acts unlike a quantifier in the following examples, but these do not, as far as I know, offer evidence as to what the correct analysis of "both" should be.

In (9) and (10) the intended reading is the one on which the subject NP refers to the same set of men as the object NP.

(9) a. All the men hate the others (of the men).

    b. Each of the men hates the others (of the men).

    c. *Both the men hate the other(s) (of the men).

(10) a. All the men hate each other.

    b. Each man hates each other.

    c. *Both the men hate each other.

(11) a. *All Tom, Dick, and Harry left.

    b. Both Tom and Dick left.

    c. Tom, Dick, and Harry all left.

3.3 Predicate "Both"

So far we have considered cases where "both" modified NPs, and found a rough balance of evidence between the quantifier and non-quantifier analyses. The quantifier analysis, however, takes a fatal blow when we observe that "both" can also modify a wide range of other types of constituent—verbs, verb phrases, adjectives, adverbs, prepositional phrases—which we shall vaguely call "predicates."[3]

(12) a. John both danced and sang a lot.

    b. Ellen both played the lyre and danced a jig.

---

[3] After this paper was presented at the Chicago Linguistic Society meeting (April 1970), it was pointed out that Green (1969) argues for a relationship between "both" and "too" using essentially the same predicate "both" evidence I use in section 3.3. Similar examples are also found in the NED.

    c.   Jane is both blond and beautiful.

    d.   The machine computes both swiftly and accurately.

    e.   John will run both in the mile and in the two-mile.

True quantifiers do not share this property:

(13)   *John all danced, jumped, and sang a lot.

    b.   *Ellen many played the lyre, danced a jig, skipped rope . . .

    c.   *Jane is each short, fat, and ugly.

    d.   *The machine computes all swiftly, accurately, and inexpensively.

    e.   *John will run every in the mile, in the half, and in the two-mile.

If the NP-modifying "both" discussed in the previous sections is a quantifier, it must be unrelated to the predicate-modifying "both" in (12). On the other hand, if "both" is derived from sentence conjunction, there should be no serious difficulty in explaining its ability to modify both NPs and predicates.

4. Proposed Solution

The evidence we have seen so far appears to lead to a contradiction: section 2 suggests that "both" is a quantifier; section 3 suggests that "both" is derived from sentence conjunction. The weight of evidence favors the sentence-conjunction hypothesis, and in the following section I shall argue that a sentence-conjunction analysis will also account for the data that originally motivated the quantifier hypothesis.

If sentences with "both" are to be derived from an underlying sentence-conjunction, we shall need a rule of *Both*-Formation (BF), which should presumably be a variant of the Conjunction-Reduction rule. While the exact form of the Conjunction-Reduction rule remains a subject for debate, its over-all characteristics have not changed greatly from Chomsky's *Syntactic Structures* statement:[4]

If S_1 and S_2 are grammatical sentences, and S_1 differs from S_2 only in that X appears in S_1 where Y appears in S_2 (i.e. $S_1 = \ldots X \ldots$ and $S_2 = \ldots Y \ldots$), and X and Y are constituents of the same type in S_1 and S_2 respectively, then S_3 is a sentence, where S_3 is the result of replacing X by $X + and + Y$ in S_1 (i.e. $S_3 = \ldots X + and + Y \ldots$).

[4] Chomsky (1957) p 36, compare Gleitman (1965) and Smith (1969).

A first approximation to BF results if we replace "$X+and+Y$" in Chomsky's rule with "$both+X+and+Y$." Of course it will be necessary to specify the derived structure output more precisely, and we shall need a mechanism to derive plurals with appropriate referential indexing from conjunctions of the same noun:[5]

the man$_i$ and the man$_j$ $\Rightarrow$ the men$_{\{i,\ j\}}$

5. Confirming Evidence

It is clear that the proposed analysis using *Both*-Formation will handle the data in sections 3.1 and 3.3. The question is whether it can also account for the evidence that originally motivated the quantifier analysis (sections 2.1 and 2.2). In the following sections we take up first the surface and then the deeper parallels between "both" and the quantifiers; we shall see that the proposed analysis can handle both, and that the apparatus we use would be needed in any case just to handle cases where "both" modified predicates.

5.1 Surface-Structure Parallels

In section 2.1 we saw that NP-modifying "both" appeared in a quantifier-like surface structure and was subject to the Quantifier-Moving rules. We can account for these surface-structure facts if we assume that BF applies before the Quantifier-Moving rules and produces the same derived structure as Quantifier Lowering.[6] BF will then produce the quantifier-like structure of (2a) directly, and the Quantifier-Moving rules will subsequently move "both" into its surface-structure positions in (2b) and (2c). The problem is to justify this proposal to graft the surface structure of the quantifier analysis onto the rival sentence-conjunction analysis.

We know that the predicate-modifying "both" (section 3.3) could not possibly come from an underlying quantifier. Thus, if we could show that predicate "both," like NP "both," act like quantifiers in surface structure, that would be substantial justification for combining a quantifier surface structure with the sentence-conjunction analysis.

Fortunately the First Quantifier-Moving rule (QMl) provides just such

---

[5] This requirement leads to serious but apparently unavoidable difficulties. See footnote 10, and McCawley (1968) p 144ff.

[6] Since the details of QL's derived-structure output are an open question, the claim being made here is that, whatever the derived structure of Quantifier Lowering turns out to be, the derived structure for BF will be the same.

evidence. This rule moves a quantifier around the NP it modifies:

All the boys left $\xrightarrow{\text{QMl}}$ The boys all left.

It applies most freely to quantifiers modifying subject NP, but it also applies to certain quantifiers modifying NP in sentence-final position:[7]

    (14) a. The marksman missed the targets—every one of them.

           b. God bless us all.

Most important, it applies to "both" modifying sentence-final NP conjunctions:

    (15) a. Higewulf danced with Sally and Sue both.

           b. The marksman hit the gold and the red targets both.

We must therefore predict that QMl will also apply to "both" modifying sentence-final predicate conjunctions. This is indeed the case:

    (16) a. John both danced and sang.

           b. John danced and sang both.

    (17) a. The machine computes both swiftly and accurately.

           b. The machine computes swiftly and accurately both.

    (18) a. John will run both in the mile and in the two-mile.

           b. John will run in the mile and in the two-mile both.

Plainly the same rule is operating in the NP and predicate cases, and the quantifier derived structure proposed for BF is therefore confirmed.

5.2   Deeper Parallels

Equi-NP Deletion and *Not*-Transportation operate before Quantifier-Lowering, so the observation that BF produces the same derived structure as QL will not help to explain the quantifier-like properties of "both" under Equi and *Not*-Transportation (section 2.2). The explanation, if we can find one, must be implicit in the pre-BF sentence-conjunction underlying structure of "both." In the following sections we shall see that the sentence-conjunction structure does account for the behavior of "both" under Equi, at least within the limits of our present knowledge of anaphora, and also for its behavior under *Not*-Transportation.

5.2.1   Equi-NP Deletion

    (19)   is a semantically plausible underlying structure for (4a):

---

[7] Sse Carden (1968a) p 20, 23–7.

(19)   Both the candidates expect both the candidates to win.

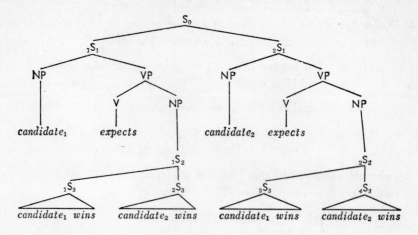

If Equi-NP Deletion is ordered before BF, it will be blocked. BF can then apply in S_2 and S_0, giving the desired surface structure (21).

(20)

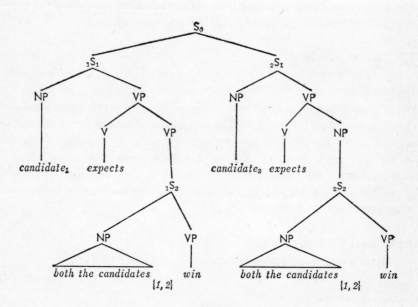

(21)

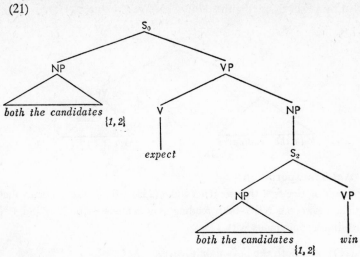

(22) is a semantically plausible underlying structure for (4b):

   (22)   Both the candidates expect to win.

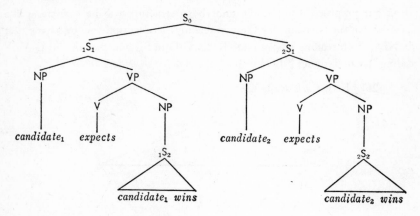

Equi-NP Deletion will apply in S_1:

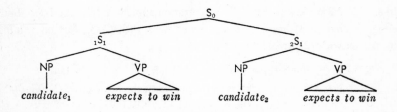

Followed by BF in S_0, giving the desired surface structure (24):

(24)

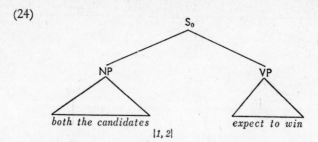

5.2.2 *Not*-Transportation

We should notice first that sentences like (25a) are (at least in many dialects) ambiguous between a NEG-Both reading synonymous with (25b) and a NEG-Verb reading synonymous with (25c).

(25) a. Both the boys didn't leave.
      b. It is not the case that both the boys left.   (NEG-Both)
      c. Both the boys stayed.   (NEG-Verb)

Given our proposed analysis, the underlying structure will be something like (26). We can then account for the two readings in a natural way by saying that the NEG-Both reading has an underlying NEG in S_0, and that the NEG-Verb reading has underlying NEGs in both the S_1s.

(26) Both the boys left.

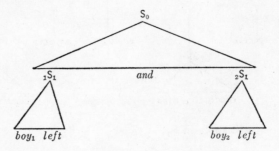

In section 2.2 we saw that *Not*-Transportation applied only to the NEG-Both reading, so that (27a) has a reading synonymous with (27b), but no reading synonymous with (27c):

(27) a. I don't think both the boys left.
      b. I think it is not the case that both the boys left.   (NEG-Both)
      c. I think both the boys stayed.   (NEG-Verb)

If we order *Not*-Transportation before BF,[8] the fact that (27a) has only the NEG-Both reading follows directly from the well-known observation that *Not*-Transportation can take a NEG only from the topmost embedded S. When the structure of (26) is embedded under "I think," a NEG in S_0, as in the NEG-Both reading, is available for *Not*-Transportation, while a NEG in S_1 is not.

As in section 5.1, the use of the sentence-conjunction analysis is confirmed by the observation that predicate-modifying "both" act just like the NP-modifying "both" in (4a) and (27a):

(28)   I don't think John both danced and sang.

(28) has a NEG-Both reading, but not NEG-Verb reading.

It is important to notice that the conjunction underlying "both" appears in a "higher S" and can be semantically negated, and thus has two of the crucial properties of "higher predicates" like true quantifiers.

6.   Conclusion and Speculation

This appendix began with an attempt to resolve an apparent contradiction between evidence that "both" was a quantifier and evidence that "both" came from an underlying sentence conjunction. The weight of evidence favored the sentence-conjunction hypothesis, and we have just seen that a suitable sentence-conjunction analysis will also account for the quantifier-like properties of "both." We conclude that "both" represents an underlying conjunction with some of the properties of a "higher predicate."

Certain serious problems remain untouched by our analysis.[9] The partial similarities between "both" and "each" raise difficulties that I cannot discuss at this time.[10] Likewise, the similarities in derived structure output and order

---

[8] Notice that we have now required BF to follow Equi-NP Deletion and *Not*-Transportation, and to precede the Quantifier-Moving rules. The ordering of BF is thus the same as that of Quantifier-Lowering with respect to all the rules we have considered.

[9] Moreover, a good supply of problems remains unmentioned. For example, there is substantial unaccounted-for idiolect variation on the grammaticality of sentences like (F2):

(F2)   *Both the men$_i$ hate both the men$_i$.

Or consider the relation of "both" to "respective":

(F3)   a.   Both Tom and Dick love their respective wives.
       b.   *Both Tom and Dick love Jane and Bronwyn respectively.

[10] McCawley has proposed (1968 p 152) that NPs with set indices (i.e. semantic plurals) be subcatagorized into /+joint/, appearing with *together* etc., and /−joint/, appearing with *each* etc. At first glance it would seem to be possible to extend this analysis to *both* and so keep *both* as an underlying quantifier. Certain problems arise, however, if this is attempted:

1.   There is no natural way to account for the fact that *both the men* means exactly two

between BF and Quantifier-Lowering, though motivated by the behavior of predicate-modifying "both," remain unexplained. Further, in a system with derivational constraints, the facts about *Not*-Transportation would be handled by the same derivational constraint used for quantifiers, and indeed George Lakoff has found independent evidence that such a derivational constraint applies to both quantifiers and conjunctions.[11] All this suggests that a wider generalization should be sought, in which quantifiers and conjunctions (and perhaps negatives) would form a natural class of "logical predicates." It should then be possible to find a principled explanation for those similarities between conjunctions and quantifiers which seem accidental in our present analysis.

men, which would follow directly from the BF rule and appropriate constraints on iteration. One might argue that this could be handled by ths same mechanism that produces dual, trial, or paucal number in other languages, but this would fail to explain the fact that the predicate *both* also requires a group of two predicates.

2. The whole relation between predicate *both* and NP *both* remains unexplained.

3. Restriction to co-occurrence with /−joint/ NPs would not by itself explain any of the unquantifier-like properties of *both*, since some quantifiers appear with both /+joint/ and /−joint/ NPs, and *each* (which would have to be a quantifier in this analysis) is restricted to /−joint/ NPs.

    (F4)   a.   All the men left together.   /+joint/
             b.   All the professors are erudite.   /−joint/
             c.   *Each of the men left together.   /+joint/

It therefore appears that the McCawley analysis, even if correct for *each*, cannot be extended to *both*. This leaves us in the unesthetic position of claiming that the /−joint/ properties of *each* and the /−joint/ readings of plural noun phrases are determined in one way, while apparently identical properties of *both* are determined in quite another.

We saw above that the McCawley analysis of *each* cannot be extended to *both*; we might now ask if it is possible to extend the sentence-conjunction analysis of *both* to include *each* and other /−joint/ plurals. There are two main arguments against this:

a. McCawley points out that deriving /−joint/ reading of plurals from sentence conjunctions involves very large deep structures, e.g. a deep structure of 10 million sentences for (F5a). Worse, there are examples where no well-defined number of underlying sentences would give the desired result (F5b).

    (F5)   a.   Ten million Chinese are erudite.
             b.   Roughly 500 linguists understand deep structure.

Restriction of the sentence-conjunction analysis to *each* doesn't help, since *each* can appear with the most offensive sort of NP:

    (F6)   Approximately one billion Chinese each love Chairman Mao.

b. Such an analysis predicts that we will get a predicate *each* comparable to predicate *both*. This is of course false:

    (F6)   *John each danced, sang, skipped rope, and strummed a violin.

We are forced to conclude that, awkward though it may seem, the similar properties of *both* and *each* cannot be accounted for by the same formal mechanism in our existing theory. An explanation of whatever underlying regularity there may be will have to wait for a cleverer linguist.

[11] G. Lakoff (1970b), section 3.

Bibliography

Andrews, Avery D. (1971) "Case Agreement of Predicate Modifiers in Ancient Greek," *Linguistic Inquiry* 2: 127–51.

Bach, Emmon (1970) "Problominalization," *Linguistic Inquiry* 1: 121–2.

Bailey, Charles-James N. (1969) "The Integration of Linguistic Theory: Internal Reconstruction and the Comparative Method in Descriptive Analysis," *Working Papers in Linguistics* 2.4: 93–102.

Bailey, Charles-James N. (1970a) "A Proposed Qualification on Guy Carden's Notion of a 'Possible Sub-Dialect'," *Working Papers in Linguistics* 2.8: 31–2.

Bailey, Charles-James N. (1970b) "Using Data Variation to Confirm, Rather than Undermine, the Validity of Abstract Syntactic Structures," *Working Papers in Linguistics*, 2.8: 77–86.

Baker, C.L. (1970a) "A Note on Scope of Quantifiers and Negation," *Linguistic Inquiry* 1: 138–40.

Baker, C.L. (1970b) "Double Negatives," *Linguistic Inquiry* 1: 169–86.

Carden, Guy (1967) "Quantifiers as Higher Verbs," unpublished IBM technical report BPC 5.

Carden, Guy (1968a) "English Quantifiers," in *Mathematical Linguistics and Automatic Translation, Report NSF 20*, Computation Laboratory of Harvard University, Cambridge, Massachusetts.

Carden, Guy (1968b) "A Note on 'None'," in *Mathematical Linguistics and Automatic Translation, Report NSF 20*, Computation Laboratory of Harvard University, Cambridge, Massachusetts.

Carden, Guy (1970) "A Note on Conflicting Idiolects," *Linguistic Inquiry* 1: 281–90.

Carden, Guy (1971) "A Dialect Argument for *Not*-Transportation," *Linguistic Inquiry* 2: 423–6.

Carden, Guy and Anthony G. Miller (1970) "More Problominalizations," *Linguistic Inquiry* 1: 555–6.

Carden, Guy (1972) "Disambiguation, Favored Readings, and Variable Rules," in C-J. N. Bailey and R. W. Shuy. *New Ways of Analyzing Variation in English*, Georgetown University Press, Washington, D. C.

Carden, Guy (1973) "Dialect Variation and Abstract Syntax," in R. W. Shuy, ed., *Some New Directions in Linguistics*, Georgetown University Press, Washington, D. C.

Chomsky, Noam (1957) *Syntactic Structures*, Mouton, The Hague.

Chomsky, Noam (1965) *Aspects of the Theory of Syntax*, The MIT Press, Cambridge, Massachusetts.

Chomsky, Noam (1970) "Some Empirical Issues in the Theory of Transformational Grammar," in P. S. Peters, *Goals of Linguistic Theory*, Prentice-Hall, Englewood Cliffs, New Jersey (to appear).

DeCamp, David (1963) review of F. G. Cassidy, *Jamaica Talk*, *Language* 39: 536–44.

Elliott, Dale, Stanley Legum, and Sandra Annear Thompson (1969) "Syntactic Variation as Linguistic Data," in *Papers from the Fifth Regional Meeting of the Chicago Linguistic Society*, Department of Linguistics, University of Chicago, Chicago, Illinois.

Fillmore, Charles (1963) "The Position of Embedding Transformations in a Grammar," *Word*, 19: 208–31.

Gleitman, Lila R. (1965) "Co-ordinating Conjunctions in English," *Language* 41: 260–93.

Green, Georgia M. (1969) "Some Theoretical Implications of the Lexical Expression of Emphatic Conjunction," unpublished paper, University of Chicago, Chicago, Illinois.

Grinder, John, and Paul Postal (1971) "Missing Antecedents," *Linguistic Inquiry* 2: 289–312.

Halle, Morris (1962) "Phonology in Generative Grammar," *Word* 18: 54–72; reprinted in Fodor and Katz, *Readings in the Philosophy of Language*, Prentice-Hall, Englewood Cliffs, New Jersey, 1964.

Heringer, James T. (1970) "Research on Quantifier-Negative Idiolects," in *Papers from the Sixth Regional Meeting of the Chicago Linguistic Society*, Department of Linguitics, University of Chicago, Chicago, Illinois.

Hockett, Charles F. (1955) *A Manual of Phonology*, Waverly Press, Baltimore, Maryland.

Horn, Laurence R. (1970) "Ain't it hard (anymore)," in *Papers from the Sixth Regional Meeting of the Chicago Linguistic Society*, Department of Linguistics, University of Chicago, Chicago, Illinois.

Jackendoff, Ray S. (1968a) "Quantifiers as Noun Phrases," in *Studies in Transformational Grammar and Related Topics*, Air Force Document AFCRL–68–0032, Bedford, Massachusetts; reprinted in *Foundations of Language* 4: 422–42.

Jackendoff, Ray S. (1968b) "On Some Incorrect Notions about Quantifiers and Negation," in *Studies in Transformational Grammar and Related Topics*, Air Force Document AFCRL–68–0032, Bedford, Massachusetts.

Jackendoff, Ray S. (1969a) *Some Rules for English Semantic Interpretation*, MIT PhD. Thesis. See also Jackendoff (1972).

Jackendoff, Ray S. (1969b) "An Interpretive Theory of Negation," *Foundations of Language* 5: 218–41.

Jackendoff, Ray S. (1971) "On Some Questionable Arguments about Quantifiers and Negation," *Language* 47: 282–97 (a revised version of Jackendoff 1968b).

Jackendoff, Ray S. (1972) *Semantic Interpretation in Generative Grammar*, The MIT Press, Cambridge, Massachusetts.

Katz, J.J. and J.A. Fodor (1963) "The Structure of a Semantic Theory," *Language* 39: 170–210; reprinted in Fodor and Katz, *Readings in the Philosophy of Language*, Prentice-Hall, Englewood Cliffs, New Jersey 1964.

Katz, J.J. and P.M. Postal (1964) *An Integrated Theory of Linguistic Descriptions*, The MIT Press, Cambridge, Massachusetts.

Keyser, S.J. (1963) review of Hans Kurath and Raven I. McDavid, *The Pronunciation of English in the Atlantic States*, *Language* 39: 303–16.

Klima, Edward S. (1964a) "Relatedness between Grammatical Systems," *Language* 40:1–20; reprinted in Reibel and Schane, *Modern Studies in English*, Prentice-Hall, Englewood Cliffs, New Jersey, 1969.

Klima, Edward S. (1964b) "Negation in English," in J.A. Fodor and J.J. Katz, *The Structure of Language*, Prentice-Hall, Englewood Cliffs, New Jersey.

Labov, William, Paul Cohen, Clarence Robins, and John Lewis (1968) *A Study of the Non-Standard English of Negro and Puerto Rican Speakers in New York City*, Cooperative

Research Project No. 3288, Columbia University, New York.

Labov, William (1970) "The Study of Language in its Social Context," *Studium Generale* 23: 30–87.

Labov, William (1972) *Sociolinguistic Patterns,* University of Pennsylvania Press, Philadelphia.

Lakoff, George (1965) *On the Nature of Syntactic Irregularity, Mathematical Linguistics and Automatic Translation, Report NSF* 16, Computation Laboratory of Harvard University, Cambridge, Massachusetts.

Lakoff, George (1967) "Deep and Surface Grammar," unpublished paper, Harvard University, Cambridge, Massachusetts.

Lakoff, George (1969) "On Derivational Constraints," in *Papers from the Fifth Regional Meeting of the Chicago Linguistic Society,* Department of Linguistics, University of Chicago, Chicago, Illinois.

Lakoff, George (1970a) "Repartee, or A Reply to *Negation, Conjunction, and Quantifiers,*" *Foundations of Language* 6: 389–422.

Lakoff, George (1970b) "On Generative Semantics," in D.D. Steinberg and L.A. Jakobovits, *Semantics: an interdisciplinary reader in philosophy, linguistics, and psychology,* Cambridge University Press, Cambridge.

Lakoff, George (1970c) "Pronominalization, Negation, and the Analysis of Adverbs," in R. Jacobs and P. Rosenbaum, *Readings in English Transformational Grammar,* Blaisdell-Ginn, Boston, Massachusetts.

Lakoff, George (1970d) *Irregularity in Syntax,* Holt, Rinehart and Winston, New York, New York. (a revised version of Lakoff 1965).

Lakoff, George (1970e) "Global Rules," *Language* 46: 627–39.

Lakoff, George and Stanley Peters (1966) "Phrasal Conjunction and Symmetric Predicates," in *Mathematical Linguistics and Automatic Translation, Report NSF* 17, Computation Laboratory of Harvard University, Cambridge, Massachusetts.

Lakoff, Robin (1969a) "A Syntactic Argument for Negative-Transportation," in *Papers from the Fifth Regional Meeting of the Chicago Linguistic Society,* Department of Linguistics, University of Chicago, Chicago, Illinois.

Lakoff, Robin (1969b) "Some Reasons Why There Can't be Any *Some-Any* Rule," *Language* 45: 608–15.

Lakoff, Robin (1970) "Another Non-Source for Comparatives," *Linguistic Inquiry* 1: 128–9.

Langacker, R.W. (1969) "On Pronomianlization and the Chain of Command," in D.A. Reibel and S.A. Schane, *Modern Studies in English,* Prentice-Hall, Englewood Cliffs, New Jersey.

Lees, Robert B. (1961) "Grammatical Analysis of the English Comparative Constructicn," *Word* 17: 171–85.

McCawley, James D. (1968) "The Role of Semantics in a Grammar," in E. Bach and R.T. Harms, *Universals in Linguistic Theory,* Holt, Rinehart and Winston, New York, New York.

McCawley, James D. (1970) "Where Do Noun Phrases Come From?" in Jacobs and Rosenbaum, *Readings in Transformational Grammar,* Ginn and Ccmpany, Waltham, Massachusetts.

Miller, Richard W. (1967) "Specificity and Determiners," unpublished paper, Harvard University.

NED (1888) *A New English Dictionary on Historical Principles* = *The Oxford English Dictionary*, Clarendon Press, Oxford.

Partee, Barbara Hall (1970) "Negation, Conjunction and Quantifiers," *Foundations of Language* 6 : 153–65. (Presented at the Conference on Mathematical Linguistics, Budapest-Baltonzabadi, Hungary, Sept. 1968)

Postal, Paul (1970) "On Coreferential Complement Subject Deletion," *Linguistic Inquiry* 1 : 439–500.

Ross, John Robert (1966) "Adjectives as Noun Phrases," in D. A. Reibel and S. A. Schane, *Modern Studies in English*, Prentice-Hall, Englewood Cliffs, New Jersey (1969).

Ross, John Robert (1967) "Auxiliaries as Main Verbs," unpublished paper, MIT.

Ross, John Robert (1968) "A Note on Command," in *Mathematical Linguistics and Automatic Translation, Report NSF* 20, Computation Laboratory of Harvard University, Cambridge, Massachusetts.

Ross, John Robert, and David M. Perlmutter (1970) "A Non-Source for Comparatives," *Linguistic Inquiry* 1 : 127–8.

Saporta, Sol (1965) "Ordered Rules, Dialect Differences, and Historical Processes," *Language* 41 : 218–24.

Smith, Carlota S. (1961) "A Class of Complex Modifiers in English," *Language* 37 : 342–65.

Smith, Carlota S. (1964) "Determiners and Relative Clauses in a Generative Grammar of English," *Language* 40 : 37–52.

Smith, Carlota S. (1969) "Ambiguous Sentences with *And*," in D.A. Reibel and S.A. Schane, *Modern Studies in English*, Prentice-Hall, Englewood Cliffs, New Jersey.

Stockwell, Robert (1959) "Structural Dialectology: A Proposal," *American Speech* 34 : 258–68; reprinted in Allen and Underwood, *Readings in American Dialectology*, Appleton-Century-Crofts, New York, New York, 1971.

Trager, G.L. and H.L. Smith (1951) *An Outline of English Structure*, Studies in Linguistics: Occasional Papers 3, Norman, Oklahoma.

Vogt, Eric E. (1971) "Catalan Vowel Reduction and the Angled Bracket Notation," *Linguistic Inquiry* 2 : 233–7.

Weinreich, Uriel (1954) "Is a Structural Dialectology Possible?" *Word* 10 : 388–400; reprinted in Allen and Underwood, *Readings in American Dialectology*, Appleton-Century-Crofts, New York, New York, 1971.

Index